Just a Girl

SCARLETT JONES
with Linda Watson-Brown

mᗺ

MIRROR BOOKS

KU-787-655

First published by Mirror Books in 2020

Mirror Books is part of Reach plc
10 Lower Thames Street
London EC3R 6EN

www.mirrorbooks.co.uk

© Scarlett Jones

The rights of Scarlett Jones to be identified as the author
of this book have been asserted, in accordance with the
Copyright, Designs and Patents Act 1988.

All rights reserved. No part of this publication may be reproduced, stored in a
retrieval system, or transmitted, in any form or by any means without the prior
written permission of the publisher, nor be otherwise circulated in any form of
binding or cover other than that in which it is published and without a similar
condition being imposed on the subsequent purchaser.

Print ISBN 978-1-913406-01-1
eBook ISBN 978-1-913406-02-8

Typeset by Danny Lyle

Printed and bound in Great Britain by
CPI Group (UK) Ltd, Croydon, CR0 4YY

A CIP catalogue record for this book is available from the British Library.

Every effort has been made to fulfil requirements with regard to
reproducing copyright material. The author and publisher will be
glad to rectify any omissions at the earliest opportunity.

1 3 5 7 9 10 8 6 4 2

Cover images: Trevillion and iStock

To my children – you gave me the strength
to carry on and you are my reason to live.
You will always be my everything.

Prologue

The blows rained down on me – as they always did. He seemed like a man possessed – as he always did. My body was aching, screaming out for mercy – as it always did.

I knew there was nothing I could do to stop this. He was the one who chose when it happened, and all I could do was wait it out. I was only a teenager and yet this was my life. It had been my life for so long and I had never been able to choose. I went from beating to beating, kicked and punched, used and abused. When it wasn't happening, I was living in fear of it happening and of how much it would hurt. That pain and that fear coloured every moment of my life.

'You whore! How dare you act like this?' he screamed at me. 'How dare you not do what I say? How dare you think you have any say in this! How dare you show me up in front of my friends! Whore, whore, whore!'

Whatever I was, he had made me that way. I did everything for him, no matter how disgusting, no matter how degrading. I could never anticipate whether those things would be the right ones, but even in the few moments when he treated me as a human being, I knew it would always revert to this. I would dance to his every command, my broken body just a vessel for him to use. He didn't see me as a person, as a woman, I was just a thing. A thing that he despised but who he kept in his life because she could sometimes be of use to him. And all the time I hoped for a glimmer of something – not love, that would be too much to hope for, but maybe something close to humanity.

And him? Ed?

He was my boyfriend, my partner. He was the one who should have cared for me, who should have loved me – instead, he was my worst nightmare. He was also the father of my child. But I knew better than most how little that meant. How fathers could be the ones who would wreck your life, rip you apart and leave you open to other predators who would come along and continue the cycle. This treatment had coloured my days since childhood and it seemed as if there was never going to be a way out.

'You are nothing!' Ed screamed at me. 'Nothing!' His face contorted with anger and hatred as he continued to kick and punch my wretched body. 'Do you hear me? Do you hear me? You are worthless. You are less than the dirt on my shoes.'

'Please, Ed, please . . .' I wept.

'Shut up! Shut up!' he yelled back. Then he stopped. He finally stopped. Crouching down beside me on the filthy floor, he held my face in his hand. A jaw long broken. A nose that had gone the same way. Bruises and cuts and welts.

'You disgust me,' he hissed. 'You are nothing, do you understand? You are nothing. You – you are just a girl, a stupid whore of a girl.'

With that, he let my face drop from his hands and walked out of the room, slamming the door behind him. Every part of me ached, but it was my heart that felt it most. This shouldn't be my life, this shouldn't be anyone's life. His words rattled around in my head – *just a girl, just a girl.* That's all I had ever been to men, wasn't it? From my father onwards, I was nothing more. I was only there to be something for them to inflict pain upon.

I knew that wouldn't be the last time I would be kicked like an animal, but I truly believe that it was the moment when something changed in my mind. Perhaps it was overload. Perhaps my body had taken so much that, subconsciously, a little voice had said to me, *just get out alive – get out alive and you can do anything.*

I dragged myself up, feeling blood drip down my face from a gash at the side of my head, old and new bruises mingling together and creating a pulse throughout every inch of my body. I was filthy, aching from it all, terrified of more days and nights like these.

But I'd heard that voice for the first time. It wasn't telling me I was worthless or a whore. It wasn't telling me that this would never change. It had finally woken up and was saying, *sometimes, it takes a girl to change the world.*

Chapter One

Fine. Normal.

It's hard to look back – to try and get an idea of where you came from, where everything began, when you know where it's all going to end up, but I'll try.

I was born in 1970 and I know that I was meant to be called Lorraine up until Mum went into hospital to have me. She was reading 'Gone with the Wind' on the maternity ward and decided that Lorraine was no good at all – her little girl would be called Scarlett. It was a dramatic name for an ordinary baby in an ordinary family, and I was the only one amongst us who had such a huge character to live up to, but that was how I came to be me, and that was how there was a Scarlett in the middle of the West Midlands in the 1970s.

By the time I arrived, there were already two siblings waiting for me. All three of us had been born in London, but we moved to Telford when I was just a toddler. I don't really have many memories of London. However, there is one thing that sticks in my mind that happened before I went to school. I went to a café one day, just with Mum, and I was sitting eating some crisps while watching people play on a one-armed bandit. I couldn't take my eyes off it – this thing seemed to be giving them money for nothing! As soon as no one was standing at the machine and Mum was distracted chatting to someone, I went over, desperate to know where all this cash was coming from, and stuck my arm up inside. Sadly, I didn't get any coins and I also didn't get my arm back! I was still standing there, crisps in one hand, arm up inside the money machine, when the Fire Brigade arrived.

There is a gap in my memory for quite a while after that – I guess it is one that would stay with you! – until the next time my curiosity got the better of me. We had moved to a farm cottage in Telford where Dad was a farmhand and Mum stayed at home with us. I don't really remember anything of their lives other than that, but I do remember the stories I heard about how they had got together. Dad was from Shrewsbury and had met Mum when he was home on a visit from the Army. He was only 17, but pretended he was four years older as Mum was 21 and he didn't want her to think that he was too young. She had had a boyfriend before, an American guy, but that hadn't lasted long. They were seen as a lovely couple - he was a nice guy and everyone liked them.

To us, Mum in particular was a bit distant, but she seemed popular enough with other people. She was a very well turned out woman and always dressed in twinsets and skirts, or even suits at times, looking like she worked in an office rather than being a stay-at-home mum. She enjoyed having her bright blonde (dyed) hair blow-dried into the bouffant styles of the time when we had the money for that but she also spent a lot of time trying to backcomb it herself with a fag hanging out of her mouth. I used to think she would set herself on fire one day! Mum was a tiny little woman, with dainty hands and feet that were always perfectly manicured – and she had a different face for different people too. The life and soul when the mood took her, and a great one to stand around and gossip with the other women, but, as a mother, she was completely disinterested. Actually, disinterest was on a good day, but I'm getting ahead of myself here.

Dad's background had always been a bit hazy, but he was from a huge family. I absolutely loved the big get-togethers that happened every so often where there would easily be 40 people there, usually at the house of Dad's parents. I particularly loved Dad's sister, Auntie Sarah. She was the Marilyn Monroe of Shrewsbury! Slim, always perfectly made-up, she dressed like a film star and I dreamed of being like her one day. He was quite a short man, dark-haired and usually with a moustache or beard depending on the fashion, and, like Mum, he was either well-dressed if there was anyone to impress, or a complete scruff if not.

I started school in the year above as there was no space in the classes for five-year-olds. It meant that I had to do that year twice but I was a happy child with a straightforward life, and school was easy too. At that point, I was living on a farm with fields as my playground. I would run through them on my own, completely safe, with my imagination making castles of the hay bales, with the sun shining down all summer long. We all tend to think that summers back then were always glorious, but I genuinely do only remember the weather being like that. I'd play outside whenever I could, running home at the end of the day, little tanned legs, sticky face from the picnic in a bag I'd taken with me, and ready to collapse with tiredness from fresh air and playing. I'd sometimes be with my siblings, sometimes with neighbouring children from a few miles away, sometimes on my own – but there was always a feeling of freedom. There was a canal nearby where we'd try to catch fish – I'm not sure there were any in there, to be honest! – and old farm buildings in which we could play hide and seek. It was idyllic. We even used to hitchhike into the local town with Mum if we needed anything from the shops, and that wasn't frowned upon, it was just a natural thing to do back then.

We didn't have much money, but life was happy enough at that stage, I guess. You don't know any different when you're little. Mum did hit us for as far back as I could remember, and she was vicious, but it was just part of life. I can't recall a time when she wasn't muttering or shouting 'fucking kids' at us. We never seemed to bring her much joy, just misery and annoyance.

When I was six, we moved away from the farm, back into town to a miserable council house. I would walk to my new school with my sister and the new friend I'd made who lived next door to us, but I missed the open fields and the sense of freedom I'd had living on the farm. At that age, I was still going with the flow really and, back then, children would never have made a fuss about things that brought any sort of upheaval into their world or they'd get a backhanded slap. However, there was one difference to our lives that did make an impression. Mum became a foster parent.

'We're getting someone else to live with us,' she announced one day.

'Who?' I asked.

'She's called Diane – she's older than you. She's a teenager,' Mum informed me.

'What's she coming for? Why's she living with us?' I probed.

'None of your business really,' she shot down. 'I've decided to foster. I'm going to be a mum to other kids too.'

Again, I just accepted it, but couldn't particularly understand why she'd want to be a mum to more given that she wasn't that bothered about us. It didn't seem to be her calling, she wasn't maternal at all, so I had no idea what had come over her. In retrospect, it was probably that she would get paid for it as she hadn't worked since we moved to the new area.

Dad was a taxi driver and wasn't around much as he had early starts then slept for a lot of the day, meaning there was little parental influence on my life. We certainly weren't the sort of family who played board games at night or went on laughter-filled holidays. We didn't sit down and chat about our day or have a Sunday roast to enjoy together. All Mum liked to do with us involved taking a wooden spoon to our backsides and cursing.

Diane, the foster child, didn't have much of an impact on my life either. She was quiet and stayed in her own room most of the time. She moved on after about a year which I guess was linked to the fact that we were having to move too as the house was due to get knocked down for redevelopment. However, before the plans to move became reality, Mum had another announcement for us.

'We're not going to Hadley – we're going . . . somewhere else,' she told us. 'Don't ask questions. There will be other women there, other kids, and your dad isn't coming.'

I started to do exactly what I'd been told not to and a question was forming, but she caught me quickly.

'Shut up! NO questions. Get your stuff, we're going now.'

'Can't we wait until Dad gets back?' I plucked up the courage to ask. 'He can help us shift everything.'

'Christ no,' she sighed. 'He's the shit we're getting away from. Quickly, get what you can pack and don't arse about.'

We all packed what we could into sports bags, carrier bags, anything we could find, but I didn't know where we were going. It was much later when I realised it was a women's refuge for victims of domestic abuse. Mum was antsy, constantly looking out of the window, telling us to hurry up. Dad was working long hours by then, sometimes helping his friend as a mini-van driver, but she must have felt he'd got wind of what was happening and could have turned up at any moment. I had no awareness of any violence that had been going on between them. I'd heard shouting for all of my life, and they didn't seem particularly happy, but Mum was never hit in front of me.

I'm not doubting it, I'm just saying that I was innocent of this whole aspect of relationships at that age. I never had a close bond with Mum. I don't remember any real affection, not for any of us, so she would never have confided. She was someone who clacked around the house in her high heels and suits, seeming quite content in her own way. Not as a mum, but as a person. She couldn't have been really. I never saw her crying, never saw bruises, but that means nothing. Women are good at hiding abuse, they are good at presenting a front, but what goes on behind closed doors is another matter entirely – as I would find out when I get older.

There was an atmosphere in the hostel that I have never forgotten. Yes, there was fear every time someone knocked on the door; yes, there was anxiety that caused some women to peek out from behind the curtains constantly, scanning the street. However, there was also a camaraderie. There were five families in there and the women would share their stories, they would all cook shared meals, look after each other's kids, and generally get by on what they could.

I remember that my big sister Jackie and I had chickenpox while we stayed there. There is such a clear memory in my mind of us both sitting in the bath together, absolutely covered in spots, laughing at the fact that we were the first in the hostel to catch them. It was a shared bathroom, so when the others heard us laughing they all came in for a look too! I guess it sticks in my mind as it was a genuinely happy moment. Jackie was fine throughout that time, but my brother, Joey, was already going off the rails. He'd been caught shoplifting sweets and that was just the start of what he would get up to over the years. He would actually bring the bags of sweets to Jackie and me, who would never ask questions about where they had come from, which I suppose shows that it was the act of doing something wrong that appealed to him, not what he could get out of it. Joey's story is his to tell, not mine, but he was certainly affected by having a mum who didn't care and a dad who was, at best, absent.

I'm not sure how long we had been there – just a matter of days I think – when Mum told us she was going out to meet someone.

'Who is it?' I asked.

'None of your business,' was the usual answer.

I didn't mind the refuge, but the thought of a trip out was better.

'Can I come too?' I pleaded. I watched Jackie and Joey as I asked. 'Can we all come?'

'Oh, for fuck's sake,' she sighed. 'I suppose so. Don't get your hopes up though. It's just your dad I'm seeing. Fucking kids.'

Dad! That must mean we were going home. She dragged us along reluctantly and I saw him as we turned a street corner, standing idly, smoking a cigarette. That became a pattern. They would meet up quite regularly, we'd all go to a café, then we'd head back to the refuge. I never really noticed what they were like together; they were just adults talking a lot, but I was always excited to see him.

'We're moving out,' Mum announced one day, after we'd been in the hostel for about six months. I hadn't been privy to any of the decisions that led to any move in my life so far, and this was another I just accepted. So, off we went, leaving the refuge and moving into a council house in Hadley. I had to share a bedroom with Jackie there, but it was OK. We were one in a row of houses that backed onto a park and we used to jump our fence to get to it rather than go the long way round. I was never happier than when I was outside and spent most of my free time there.

Mum dressed me and Jackie in the same clothes from as far back as I can remember. There were horrible denim dungarees, flares, flowery dresses with huge collars, each outfit more disgusting than the one before. It's these clothes I remember at that time, when I climbed over the fence, getting some bit of flowing fabric caught up in the wooden slats and cursing her for whatever outfit we had on that day. Maybe she was showing some interest in us by dressing us up, but I remember her as just there, no real personality, no real engagement with any of us. Any memories are tainted now, but there is nothing wonderful that stands out anyway. I don't have much of a sense of time at that point in my life but, at some stage, Dad moved back in. No big fuss. He was just back one day. I never saw them kissing and cuddling, and I never witnessed violence but he had come back for a reason, I assumed.

I never thought for a moment that the reason was me.

I seemed to be the only one he showed affection to, but there had been that break when we had been in the hostel and I was only six, so – again – I just accepted it. Maybe he had been like this before we left? Maybe I had just forgotten. To begin with, I loved it. He'd come in from work every day and wrap his arms round me in a huge bear hug.

'Where's my princess?' he'd ask, and I'd giggle in his arms, trying to ignore the looks of hate my mum was throwing our way. Sometimes, he would sit in his chair laughing and call out to me.

'Come sit on my lap, Princess – your old Dad's had a hard day. Come and cheer me up.'

It was fine. It was normal.

It progressed into him seeming to have a back that needed scratching every day when he got home, but there was nothing there that seemed odd. He'd lift his shirt up and tell me what a good job I was doing as my little nails tried to catch the itch.

It was fine. It was normal.

As was the violence. Mum's weapons of choice were bamboo canes or wooden spoons. Those can whack pretty well when you're a little kid. She'd make us all stand in a line when something had gone wrong – or missing. It was usually money that had been taken from her purse and it was always Joey who had taken it, but she wanted to make us all suffer.

'Who did it? Who STOLE from ME?' she'd demand to know, her voice getting more and more screechy. 'Tell me NOW! Put your hands out NOW! You fucking kids! If you don't admit it was you by the time this spoon gets to you, you'll all get it!'

We'd get it from her with the cane or the spoon anyway, and we lived in fear of her. It was unpredictable, not just related to Joey stealing, but if she thought we had backchatted or not tidied enough or been lazy. Most of it was made up so you couldn't guess how to avoid being hit and she seemed to take pleasure in that.

She would threaten us with a bigger beating from Dad when he got in but that didn't bother me. I was his princess. I was for hugs and giggles and backscratching. He could lay into the others, but he wouldn't beat me. He'd go at them with a slipper or a belt with a huge buckle on it, but I'd be sent out of the room, listening to their cries from the safety of the bedroom I shared with Jackie. She'd come up once it was all over and ask me why I had avoided it yet again.

'What makes you so special?' she'd weep. 'Why doesn't he hit you?'

I'd just shrug. I had no idea and as long as I wasn't seeing welts rise from a belt buckle or red angry marks from a leather-soled slipper, I wasn't really that bothered.

It was a mundane life. Mum had become even more distant. There was only ever negative emotion from her and she certainly never hugged me. Touching was just not done and I knew never to try. I don't know what made her so cold, I never will, but I learned from that point that Dad was the only one who would ever be tactile with me. It wasn't that she had changed from being a cuddly mum – it was that she become even more distant and he had become the one I could always snuggle up with.

But . . . that was fine.

That was my normal.

I'm looking back at that little girl now. I'm watching her from her own future and I just want to reach inside the memories and hold her tight. I'm going to be beside her every step of the way as she tells her story, from girl to teenager to woman. There's so much I'd like to tell her – to tell me – that matters. You only know these things in hindsight but they are lessons that can hopefully help others. I would tell little Scarlett to enjoy every second of her carefree life. To enjoy those trips with the school, fishing at the Ercall River. Enjoy making damson jam with your classmates. Revel in the little pleasure of sitting on the rug at story time while your friends play with your long hair and the teacher whisks you off to make-believe worlds. Make the most of joining in with every group activity because you just want to have some fun. Accept every invite to every party that your six and seven and eight-year-old friends are having. Throw yourself into those family get-togethers and tell Auntie Sarah that you want to be just like her when you're grown up. Play innocently, play freely, make the most of every moment because it's all about to change, little Scarlett – and it's a change that will affect your entire life. Stay strong and believe in yourself. I'll be here, watching, and I know that you'll make it but there are hard times ahead, little one, such hard times.

Chapter Two

Such a good girl

At this stage in my life, I only had two things that gave me real pleasure – animals (especially my cat, Whiskers), and schoolwork. Maths was the area that interested me most, and I loved solving problems and working things out. There was nothing to suggest that there was a problem I would *never* figure out on that day in 1978 when I was eight years old.

It was a normal after-school day and I was plonked on the sofa watching 'Grange Hill' when a shout came from the bathroom upstairs. By this point, although Mum still wasn't working, she had an obsession with bingo. She'd go to the afternoon session while we were at school and walk back after 5pm when it closed to get ready for the evening customers. She never seemed to be able to get to enough sessions, but they cost money and she was generally skint. I think if she could have managed it, she would have been there morning, noon and night. I quite liked that time before she'd start on us 'fucking kids' again, and 'Grange Hill' was my favourite programme by far.

Annoyance niggled at me and I ignored the first call from Dad.

'Scarlett!' he shouted again. 'Come up here a minute will you, Princess?'

I thought nothing of his demand other than it being an interruption to my telly watching. I stomped upstairs and hoped I could get back to my programme quickly. I was mardy at the thought of doing anything for him and couldn't imagine what was any more important than me watching telly. It was a small, funny shaped bathroom with the handbasin on the diagonal and the loo in the middle with the bath along a wall. The suite was white with black sides, and there was a shower attachment which went onto the taps with bits of rubber which often flew off with a whoosh of water when you least expected.

I didn't know anyone with a proper shower back then and even the rubber taps were quite a new development and we felt kind of posh having them.

The door was ajar when I got there and Dad called my name again.

'Scarlett? You took your time. Come in here a second, get a move on!'

I thought nothing of it as I pushed the door ajar.

'Yeah? What d'you want?'

Dad put his head around the side of the plastic, palm tree adorned shower curtain. It was a house of the 70s, that's for sure.

'Pass me the soap from the sink love, will you? Don't want to risk coming out for it or those bloody rubber taps will come off again.'

I knew the feeling. Any time I had tried to use them, there was no warning before the pressure built up and they whacked off from the main taps, splattering the whole bathroom with water. All I wanted was to get back to 'Grange Hill' – Tucker and the gang could be getting up to anything while I wasn't watching! I stuck my hand out with the bar of green marbled Shield soap in it.

'Do me a favour, Princess – give your old dad's back a good scrub, will you? Sitting too long in that bloody taxi – I'm all aches and pains.'

I sighed dramatically. Quicker I did this, quicker I could get back to the telly. I lathered up my hands and started washing him quickly, as his back was to me. But then, with no warning, he turned around. God, if I wasn't careful, I'd see everything! My hands were still lathered up when, inexplicably, he took them in his and started to rub them over his own body, keeping eye contact with me the whole time.

'Dad!' I snapped. 'What are you doing?'

'Sssh,' he whispered. 'It's fine – just help me out, Princess.'

I'd actually seen him naked before as both my parents used to walk around with no clothes on quite regularly, but I used to just avert my eyes. I couldn't do that now – and the touching was new. I'd had to scratch his back before, but this . . . this was something I hadn't been prepared for.

'Why would you want me to wash you, Dad? You can do that yourself. I need to get back downstairs,' I protested.

'Ssh, ssh,' he hissed. 'Just a minute, just stay a minute. There's no one in is there?' I shook my head. 'Good, good.' His hands were clamped on mine and, although I tried to wriggle them free, I had no choice but to be guided by his as he made me touch him all over, showing me what to do. I couldn't for the life of me understand why he would want me to do this. Why did he not just have a shower himself? He wasn't disabled, he hadn't hurt himself — why?

The strangest thing was, he was acting as if this was something so nice, so enjoyable. If that was the case, why did I feel sick? This was my dad. This was a man's private parts. My *dad's* private parts. I didn't want to touch those! I wouldn't have known what ejaculation was back then, but, in retrospect, I do know that he didn't get to that stage on that occasion. I guess he had what he wanted. He'd made me touch him in the most private of ways, the most inappropriate of ways, and knew now that I hadn't actually screamed or really reacted in a way that would make him terrified to do it again.

It was disgusting, but I thought it was a one-off. He was tired, he was working long hours — he'd just needed someone to help him as, in my eyes, he was ancient after all. Old people often needed help with things and maybe he had just made a mistake when I had helped him wash his back?

I went back to the TV but 'Grange Hill' was over. I didn't know it, but so was my childhood. I couldn't quite process what had happened and think that I probably went into a state of denial. That couldn't possibly have been what had gone on, could it? Dad wouldn't have taken my hands and made me do that? Why was I thinking such things? What on earth had made my mind get it all so twisted? The longer I sat there, the more I thought that it was me who was mixed up. Paedophiles are good at that. They are experts in making a child question not what has been done to that child by them, but what *they* got wrong, what *they* did to make it happen, or what *they* aren't remembering properly. The more I pondered it, the more I told myself that it couldn't have been a big deal. That meant that it wasn't something I would mention to Mum, or anyone else.

When Dad came downstairs about twenty minutes later, I was still on the sofa, staring at the TV but not really watching anything. Mum was in the kitchen by then, throwing together something for tea, and I didn't look at him as he walked in.

'Alright Princess?' he asked.

I nodded.

'You're a good girl, you really are. Here you go – buy yourself some sweets,' he said, closing my hand over a ten pence coin. He kissed me on the cheek as if he was just a kindly father, giving me a bit of extra pocket money for doing some chores. He'd tested the water and found it to be absolutely fine. In fact, it was so fine that it happened once a week for six months. I always got my ten pence afterwards for sweets. I always got my payment. It eventually felt like it was just something that happened to me, something that went on regularly, but I was also noticing that I was in the bathroom for longer as time went on. Dad wasn't as happy with me as quickly as he had been at the start. He would still guide my hands over him but there would be times when he would say, quite crossly, that I should go. I didn't get 10p at times like that.

After those six months, he obviously decided that he needed more. My hands would be put on his private parts as always, but he started moving them up and down much more vigorously. He would make me grasp it and do this strange movement that he wanted.

'That's it, that's a good girl,' he would gasp. 'That's my princess.'

Then, it was as if there was more soap on my hands. I had no idea what that was back then, no idea at all what was happening to me. This wasn't something that had been taught to me at school, I was too young for sex education. I honestly thought that it was just more soap, but I didn't know why there was so much of it. I also knew that I loved him and that this made him happy, whatever it was. He would reward me with smiles and hugs that meant the world to me.

You're my princess.

You're just such a good girl to me.

You're the best girl in the world.

All of it manipulation, all of it designed to shut me up. The truth was, who would I tell? Mum wouldn't have listened, I doubt she would have believed me. I'd get her usual response of 'fucking kids', then she'd be off to bingo again. With her like that, Dad knew just how to make me love him despite what he was getting me to do. I knew

I was making him happy and as a child that's all you want. I thought I was special as he told me that during and after those hideous bathroom activities. There was now no pretence at washing his back and I thought it was all normal. Everyone helped their dad, didn't they? I just assumed it happened, just assumed this was a thing I should do. As he was making me do these things while he was standing in the bath with the shower attachment running, there wasn't even any 'evidence' on my hands.

I told myself that I could cope with it. I was a good girl, I was his princess, and this was something that he liked. But it wasn't enough for him. It's never enough for men like him. They know the end game from the start and they're just working up to it, seeing what they can get away with. I was a lamb to the slaughter. He knew that Mum was completely disinterested and that I would never confide in her as a result, and he was presenting himself as the loving parent as well as treating me differently to Joey and Jackie. Putting up barriers; it was divide and rule really. I wonder if he genuinely convinced himself that this was just what all little girls dream of? I doubt it, I doubt they do it for any other reason than their own needs and the fact that they can.

Dad used to work night shifts, go to bed in the morning once he arrived home, and get up a couple of hours after we got in from school. Mum was going to bingo more and more, and we were often left to our own devices, never knowing when she'd be there or when she would be back. It meant that I was often in the house alone, playing with my dolls, or watching telly if my favourite programmes were on. There was no option to record anything back then to watch later. If you wanted to see something, you had to be sitting there at the moment it was broadcast or you'd have missed it forever.

One day, with Mum at bingo and Dad nowhere to be seen, I'd grabbed a packet of crisps and plonked myself on the sofa as usual, vaguely watching telly but also partly wondering if I would get called up to the bathroom that day. Joey and Jackie were outside, possibly at other houses, and I was quite content. I'd had a nice day at school and only had some spelling to practice that night for a test the next day. I was good at it, not as good as I was at counting, but the prospect of a test didn't bother me at all.

I could actually hear Dad in his bedroom and thought he'd had his 'shower' by now and was getting ready for work.

Such a good girl

As I sat there, I heard a banging on the floor. That was the way that both Mum and Dad often got our attention if they wanted us to go upstairs and do something for them, but we never really jumped to it unless we were being threatened with a battering too. If it was Dad, I knew that wouldn't happen to me, so there didn't seem any rush this time.

'Scarlett! Scarlett!' he started shouting. There was no one else in the house, so I accepted it would have to be me who went up – maybe he wanted something from the kitchen, maybe he wanted me to tidy up. He wasn't in the bathroom, so that was a good sign. I didn't want to do one of his special washes today, I just wanted to enjoy the peace and quiet in the house before everyone else came in. His bedroom was at the top of the stairs and I saw him straight away.

On his bed. Completely naked. With *that thing* sticking up in the air.

'There you are,' he said, smiling. 'You took your time. Others still out playing, are they?'

Silently, I nodded.

'Good. Good. Come and sit here, Princess.' He patted the bed beside him. I was trying to just look at him, just look at his face and nothing else. I always knew I didn't

27

like it, I didn't like the stuff in the shower, but I was a good girl. If Dad told me to sit down beside him, then of course I would. He was the nice parent. Maybe it was a mistake? Maybe he'd forgotten to put a towel round him, or maybe he was feeling poorly?

'Give me your hand then, love,' he said, taking it with a gentleness that was no indicator of what was about to happen and smashing all my 'maybes' in an instant. He put his hand over mine and did the movement that usually happened in the shower.

He was grunting and panting, with his eyes closed, looking like he was going to pass out any second. He got more and more excited until lots of the stuff came out. He looked at me and said, 'do you know what that is?' I shook my head; of course I didn't. 'That's what you do for your dad, that is. Now go and get my hanky.' I knew he kept his cotton hankies in their bedside drawer, and I passed one to him. I looked at my own hand with all of that horrible muck on it. I didn't know what it was, I'd never seen it before. Was that the stuff that was like the extra soap in the shower I wondered? Why did he have soap in his thing and why did it come out when I touched it? I was utterly bewildered by it all.

'You've done a good job, Scarlett. You've made me very happy. Go back downstairs and watch your programme. I'll bring your sweetie money in a bit.'

There was still that good girl narrative that he had always stuck to, but this was different. I was disgusted and wondered at how men could possibly do such a horrible thing and couldn't imagine why they had such muck inside them. If it was soap, it was a funny kind. It smelled and was gloopy and I just wanted it away from me. I washed my hand in the bathroom next door and wondered at this new thing that didn't involve washing him.

Dad knew now that there was something else that he could get away with and he added to the campaign, the campaign against me, his own child. By the time he chose his next approach, I was starting to feel fear and anxiety every time he called my name or banged on the floor. I was eight and far too old to get bathed by an adult, but that was something he chose to ignore and it became another focus of his perverted attentions. He would stomp on his bedroom floor if Mum was out, usually after he had showered, and tell me to have a bath. At first, of course, I did – I was still obedient and I always jumped to it when

Mum told me to get one, but this wasn't the same at all. As I sat there, I desperately tried to cover myself with bubbles when he came in.

'I'm fine Dad, I can wash myself now, I'm a big girl,' I told him.

'No, you're not,' he countered. 'You're my little girl, my little princess. Now, let's see what needs doing here.' He took the bar of soap and rubbed it over his hands, making a lather the same way he always wanted me to do when he was the one being washed. The thought of him touching my body made me burn with shame, but where could I go, what could I do? Once it became clear that he wanted to use his hands on me the way he had taught me to wash him, I was terrified. He was all over me, touching everywhere. After what seemed like hours, Dad gave a big sigh and said, 'good girl Scarlett, good girl,' before leaving me in the now-cold water and going into his bedroom, closing the door of it behind him.

Quickly, I started to dread any visit to that bathroom, or indeed any request from him. No matter whether he was telling me to get in the bath or sit on the bed next to him or getting me to wash him, I was making sure I was as quick as possible. I was an eight-year-old child and I was becoming very efficient at getting my own father to ejaculate so that I could be left alone. I knew what he needed, and I knew that he expected it. It was, as awful as it sounds, my job.

The one thing I did have to look forward to was my ninth birthday party. Jackie's birthday wasn't long after mine so we always had a party in between the two dates. It wasn't anything flash, just a cake and a few friends – mostly hers, as I was becoming very wary of having anyone to ours. I preferred to go to their house and get away from anything Dad might want to do to me. It was around this time, when Jackie and I had our party, that I started to realise how anxious I was at home most of the time. I saw how natural her friends were in my house and realised I never felt carefree there any longer. Nothing happened at the party, but it was a combination of seeing those girls, knowing that I never wanted my friends at my house, and realising that their relationships with their dads were so different which all came together. It hit me that I wasn't the same as them.

There was a change at that point. I wasn't scared of Dad and I wanted to make him happy; I just wished there was another way to achieve that. I think what I was starting

31

to feel was embarrassment – and that only got worse when he took it to the next level. I was used to sitting or lying next to him, wanking him off, then one day he decided that wasn't enough.

'Take your clothes off, Princess,' he whispered.

'No, Dad!' I exclaimed.

'Go on – I want us to be the same. I've seen you before.' I didn't want to. I was hesitant but he goaded me. 'What's the difference? It's no big deal, go on, Scarlett. Do it for your Dad. It'll make me happy.'

So, I did, I took my clothes off. I felt sickened. I wasn't in the bath which made it worse – at least there was the semblance of a reason for being naked in the bath when he was there. But on his bed, in his room? Now, being there, it was feeling very wrong. I wanted to cover up and this was a different level. I always hated touching his private parts but the thought that I might feel it on my own body was nauseating. What if Mum came back? Would that be better or worse? I was sure she would blame me for something, but at least she would stop this, she wouldn't put up with this disgusting behaviour. *And in her bed*, I thought to myself. *She would go mental.*

'Lie beside me,' he said, still whispering. 'This is what all dads do, you know.' That was one of his angles. He liked to emphasise the normality of his perversions. He started to touch me and then, completely out of the blue, he did this horrible kissing thing. It was the first time he kissed me not as a dad, but as a man pretending that the child beside them wanted it to be that way. It was open-mouthed, slobbery, with his tongue probing about in me. I couldn't understand it at all but it was truly vile. Just when I thought things couldn't get worse, he started touching me. I always hated having to feel him, but I had never dreamed that he would touch me in this way. But he did – and when he started to put his fingers inside me, I just didn't have a clue what was going on.

'Just relax,' he told me, in a voice that was sounding creepier and creepier. 'It might hurt a little bit, but it'll go away if you just relax, Princess. That's my girl.'

Those fingers inside me hurt so much but, as always, I thought if I could just get through it quickly, I could get back to 'normal' life. He couldn't wait. There was no notion of building up gradually now and, suddenly, he was on top of me, crushing me, moving back and forth, and then . . . then . . . then . . . there was the most horrific pain shooting inside me.

I wanted Mum back now, I wanted her to come in shouting about what a pain in the arse I was, how kids ruined her life – I wanted her to save me.

That moment was the first time my dad raped me.

It wouldn't be the last.

I am watching this in my mind and my heart breaks for that little girl. The first thing I want to tell the me from then is that this isn't what nice, kind daddies do to their daughters. This isn't your fault, Scarlett – you have done nothing wrong and this isn't your fault. Can you be brave? Can you find a teacher or some other grown up you trust? Can you find the words to tell them? I don't know . . . how could you, how could any child? How can they find the words to say what is being done to them when they don't even know what it is? How can they say they are being raped when they don't know what rape is? How can they break the trust of their father or uncle or brother who loves them, who loves them so much, and only wants to do these things with them because it's what everyone does, isn't it? That's what we all need to remember when we are adults – a child can't explain what they don't know, what they don't comprehend. And you, Scarlett? Your world is about to get a whole lot more incomprehensible, my love.

Chapter Three

Secrets

The pain was indescribable. Even to this day, as an adult woman, I can't find the words that would actually give anyone an understanding of how bad it was. I was a tiny little thing, just turned nine years of age, and he was a grown man. It doesn't take much to imagine how traumatic it was. I can go back there in an instant. The way I couldn't catch my breath because of the weight on me. The searing pain between my legs. The disgust when he pulled out and ejaculated on my stomach. The confusion that he wouldn't stop when I cried. I didn't really know what had happened and I certainly couldn't comprehend why my dad would want to hurt me so much. I thought I was his favourite, his princess – why would he do that to someone he loved?

As soon as it was done, he seemed so pleased with himself.

'Good girl, Scarlett – good girl!' he said delightedly.

That time, he was the one who got up for a cotton hanky. He was the one who wiped it off me. That day, however, was also when he changed tack.

'Remember Princess – this is what all dads do with their little girls, but best not tell anyone. It's our secret.'

It would never have crossed my mind to tell and neither did I ask questions, I didn't ask whether he was doing the same thing with Jackie, or why I had to keep it secret if it was just what happened between daddies and daughters.

All I said was, 'I don't like it, Dad.'

'Don't you worry, Princess,' he replied, patting my leg. 'It'll be better next time. Why don't you go for a nice bath?'

I think one of the reasons I didn't ask Jackie was that I still felt that I was the chosen one. I was his favourite. I didn't want to be now. I went for a bath as he told me to, just hoping that he wouldn't come in and do anything else. I lay there, bleeding, crying, and thinking - what *was* that? I was already sure in my mind that it would happen again. Dad seemed to like it so much, why would he stop? I was shaking with pain, flooded with emotion, and thinking over and over again, *why, why, why?*

I went back to my room, put on clean clothes and did what I always did - pretended nothing had happened. Of course it happened again, just as I had suspected, but Dad did change from his usual praise – *well done, Princess, well done!* – to a new approach.

'You know that if you tell anyone about this, you'll be taken away, Scarlett? They'll blame you. They'll know all of this is your fault. You don't want that, do you?'

I shook my head. 'No, but why would they think that, Dad? Why would they say that?'

He laughed derisively. 'Come on now! It's looking at you that makes me like this. I can't help myself – and that's hardly my fault, is it? Now, be sensible. Be nice to your old Dad. It's all good, I just don't want you to get in trouble if people know you've been making me do this.'

There was a huge disconnect between, on the one hand, him saying it was all my fault and I'd get in trouble if anyone found out, and on the other what he had told me about it being completely normal and something that happened in all father-daughter relationships. The thing is, when paedophiles get children at such a young age, the child can't possibly process all of that conflicting information. They can hear completely contradictory things, but the main messages are, *it's your fault, you'll be taken away, you're to blame.* That rings in their ears with every abuse, every rape, every violation. And that becomes the soundtrack to their life.

I wondered what I could possibly be doing to bring this on. I got up, went to school, came back. I played, I watched telly, I ate my breakfast and tea, I had some toast before bed – what was it, out of all that, which drove him to do these things? And why couldn't he stop himself? He was the adult, and adults knew better, so couldn't he just decide not to do it?

The other disconnect was between what he was doing and day-to-day life, I was still going to school, still playing with friends. Mum was still belting me with spoons and sticks. I still watched telly and loved animals, enjoyed maths and read books. Not every moment of every day can be miserable, even when you are an abused child, but all of the normality is coloured by the fact that, any moment, he can call for you. Any moment, he can tell you to have a bath or pass him a bar of soap. Any moment, he can bang on the floor and tell you to take your clothes off. Any moment, he can rape you. All of those moments mean that no moment is yours. He owns it all.

Nothing was ever said by Dad outside of the bedroom or bathroom. I think that the kissing made me feel sick more than anything, the pain was something else but the kissing was vile. All of that carried on for a while, and I thought it was as far as it could go. I should have known he could always go further.

I knew that he had 'dirty' magazines in his bedside cabinet, where I was sent for his cotton hankies, but I also knew that I should never look at such things. Not for a second did I connect what happened in those with what was happening to me. When he began telling me to get the magazines out and read the 'stories' to him, I knew the words were bad and I wondered whether this was the thing that would indeed get me into trouble. This was, I know now, hardcore pornography. The images and texts showed the most appalling hatred of women, but this was what he wanted – a child reading these things to him as he lay naked on his marital bed, masturbating. He only felt himself for a little while, then I would have to take over, then he would rape me. Seeing those naked women, being touched, seeing them with open legs, made what he did to me seem normal, just as he'd always suggested it was. It didn't click that they were adults and I was a child. It was hardcore pornography normalised and the harm it did to me can never be erased. He loved it and seemed to get off on it more than anything. 'Read to me Scarlett,' he'd say, knowing that the words embarrassed me beyond belief. 'Read to me and we'll look at the nice pictures together.'

By the time I was 10, being raped was less painful. I was used to it.

Let that sink in.

By the time I was 10 years old, I had been raped so often by a grown man, by my father, that my body was used to it.

Then the next phase began. One day, I was lying on my back waiting for him to rape me when he pulled me to the end of the bed. I'd seen women put their mouths to other women in his magazines, but I could never have imagined he'd do that to me. He pulled me to the end of bed and knelt down. There was nothing more disgusting to me than the thought of what he might do as he tried to force my legs open. I tried to shut them but he was pushing and pushing at my inner thighs.

'You want this,' he told me, 'you'll like it!'

'No Dad, no I don't want it!' I told him, crying.

'Of course you do – you want to be like one of those ladies in the stories, don't you?'

It was the last thing I wanted. I knew this would hurt too. He had a beard at that point and, when he finally used enough force to get my legs open and put his face down there, I felt as if it would rip me to shreds. Why did he think of these things? How did he think of these things?

'You want to wee, don't you?' he kept saying.

'No. No, I don't.' I'd never do that.

'You do, you want to. It's fine. It's fine, Princess. Go ahead.'

I know now he wanted that as part of his perversions but I never did. I never did follow through on his wish for that horror. He raped me afterwards, after he did those things with his mouth on me – and what I could never understand as a kid was, why would you want to do that where I go for a wee? Why would you want to have your mouth down there? It confused me so much.

'Next time – my turn!' he said afterwards as if it was a party game.

He kept to his word and a few days later, he was lying on the bed, naked with me beside him, when he made his demand.

'Put your mouth on that.'

'No. I don't want to.' I should have known that those words didn't make a blind bit of difference. I'd said them plenty of times in the past. Again, I was thinking, *you wee there – you wee out of that, it's stinking!*

'Do it – be a good girl.'

He pushed my head and I gagged as it hit the back of my throat. I was actually sick at that point so he was forced to stop but then he raped me – always his default if other things didn't go to plan, or sometimes just the icing on the cake for him.

Afterwards I would usually wash, either at the sink or in the bath, and I would always get to my room as quickly as I could. I didn't watch telly so much now, I spent most of my time just staring at the wall, staring into space. I was finding my protection mode. I'd disappear to a rose-covered cottage in my mind with waves crashing on a nearby sea, waves that I could hear. I went there often when I was being raped too. I'd focus on the white woodchip ceiling in their room, trying not to smell that scent of green Shield soap. He always smelled of that and Brut aftershave, strong smells but clean ones. I still see both brands in the shops and it still knocks me for six. My little white cottage was my sanctuary, it was the life I dreamed of. I was the only one there, me and my cat. There were no grown-ups, definitely not Dad, and not even any of my aunties as they would taint my perfect world through their association with Dad. My cottage was perfect and my dissociation became perfect too.

By this point, Joey was running away a lot. Mum had plans to go back into fostering – purely for money – but, as Joey was being reported to social services for 'absconding', it meant that Mum was deemed unsuitable for family placements. They were right, of course. She couldn't even look after her own kids or keep them safe, so why should she be trusted with more? It wasn't enough to stop her though and she found a loophole by applying for children who had been taken into private care. Local authorities were much more stringent with their rules and wouldn't just hand out kids in care to anyone – with private foster-ings, they only checked an applicant once and pretty much anyone got through their system. As a result, Mum passed with flying colours.

I couldn't believe that anyone would trust more kids to her but, one day, three-year-old twins were brought to the house. Two tiny little Chinese boys who had no family in this country apart from their hardworking parents. Their Mum and Dad wanted someone to look after them as grandparents would have done in their culture so they were trying to find a foster family to help out. The mum and dad came to visit them from London every three weeks or so and I adored those boys. They were my little brothers really (and I'm still in touch with them to this day). The remarkable thing was this – Mum and Dad were amazing with them.

'I've always wanted another baby,' Mum started saying all the time, to neighbours, to us, to anyone who would listen. It was the first I'd heard of it. I have to admit though, there was something about those two little boys that brought out the best in her. The other side was that we were nothing to her after that, not that we'd ever been

45

much. She was different with them, hugging and kissing, singing songs and telling stories. Maybe it was the cash that made a difference, who knows? All I did know was that I loved them too even though they distracted her so much that there was even less chance of her noticing Dad's almost-daily attacks on me. Mum still went to bingo and Dad was all for that. He didn't find it too hard to get me when Mum was at home with the boys, but if she was out, he'd either put them to bed early or sit them in the living room with a pile of toys while he took me upstairs to be raped. I didn't really have a relationship with Jackie at this stage. I'd lost her to her own teenage years and she didn't want to be landed with me if she went out with me trying to tag along.

By the time I started Senior School at 11, I'm not sure if I ever thought about my future life. Rape and abuse had been part of my world for so long now that it was as commonplace as brushing my teeth – or having a bath. Dad was working more and more with his friend as a mini-van driver by this point and sometimes would work away, either overnight or for a few days if he was taking a party somewhere like the Blackpool Illuminations.

Although it was a huge relief, I knew it would always start again as soon as he got home, and I was spending more and more time in the rose-covered cottage in my mind.

I've often wondered if it was during his times away, or when he was on nightshift in his previous job, that Dad used to think up more ways to abuse me. He was certainly very good at it. Just when I thought he'd done everything, he'd work out another way to humiliate and hurt me.

One day he shouted for me to come up to the bedroom he shared with Mum, where – again as usual – he was lying naked, on the bed. I lay down nervously beside him, waiting to see what he wanted this time. After the vile kissing, I felt as if he was trying to push something inside of me. At first, I thought it was his fingers, but it felt different this time. He had definitely been playing with himself during whatever he was doing to me as he ejaculated on my stomach quite quickly. As usual, I was told to go and get a hanky which tended to be the signal for me to leave.

Not this time.

When I handed him the hanky, he was smiling at me. 'Here's something new for you, Princess – did you like that?'

'Did I like what?'

'This . . .' He held up a long candle.

We had a supplies box of candles and matches for the regular blackouts and power cuts that happened back then, sometimes because of storms, sometimes the whole country had them, but it was usually because Mum and Dad hadn't paid the bills. I couldn't work out why he was showing it to me – was there going to be a power cut that night?

'Take this and put it under your bed, Scarlett,' Dad said, winking at me. 'You can use it at night. Actually, take these too,' he handed me some of his hideous magazines. 'Enjoy yourself!'

'I'm not allowed matches, Dad,' I told him, 'so a candle's no use to me.' He started laughing and ruffled my hair.

'You're a funny little thing, aren't you? Candles are for more than that, you know. You had a nice time a moment ago with one, didn't you?'

I suddenly knew what he meant. He had done that, he had stuck that candle up inside me. I vowed to myself I would never use it – why would I do such a thing unless it was against my will? – but I hadn't counted on another option. Mum finding it all. I'd hidden them as far back as I could in my wardrobe but I didn't know she snooped.

'You dirty fucking slag!' she screamed when I got home from school one day. It must have been quite the find for her if she'd been put off bingo. 'You filthy fucking bitch! 11 years old and you've got this sort of muck in your room – sticking fucking candles up yourself? I can't fucking believe it!' She never questioned where I got them – and I myself have to question why that was the case.

From the moment Dad had given me the candles and the pornography, he was obsessed.

'You been doing that? Have you? You been doing that?'

I'd always lie and say I had. It was easier.

'Was it nice?'

'Yes.' Another lie. I'd do or say anything to make things as quick as possible.

'Good girl. You're a good girl, Princess.'

Wasn't I? Wasn't I such a good girl?

My period started at this time. I'd been told nothing at school, but Dad had warned me that I would bleed one day, when I was ready to become a woman. I didn't want to tell him anything about it when I found blood on my pants, so I went to Mum. She threw a book at me and sighed, saying there was all I needed about women's problems in those pages. That was it. That was my mum's caring approach to me growing up – but she must have told Dad, because that night he asked me if it was true that I'd come on.

'We'll have to use johnnies now,' he said. That was always his word for condoms. 'Can't have you getting pregnant.' I obviously knew more about sex by this point – although mostly from the school playground – but I don't think I had related it to what he did to me.

Each year, there was a big family get-together with everyone, including my beloved Auntie Sarah. At home, on Christmas morning, everything was quite mundane. We got presents, but they weren't much and I always felt that the day really began when we started the drive to Gran's house. About 30 or 40 people were always there, cousins, grandparents, aunties, uncles, and it was a much better atmosphere than at home.

After dinner, all of the men decided to go to the pub for a few hours. It was always a hectic day, and on this particular Christmas, the kids were lying on all the sofas having a nap. After a while I woke up; they were all asleep but I heard someone crying, which is what must have roused me in the first place. I crept to the kitchen where one of my cousins was crying to my mum. Valerie was older than me by quite a bit, but when you're a kid, it's hard to work out what age any grown-up is. If they're over 20, they're ancient. She was certainly married but didn't have any kids yet, and I was fond of her and her husband.

'I don't know how to stop it,' she was telling Mum, breaking her heart. 'I hate it. He comes in and rapes me whenever he wants, whenever he's near me. Please don't tell my husband. He can't ever find out.'

Mum was being quite kind, soothing her and promising she wouldn't say a word. As I listened, a shocking realisation came to me.

'I don't want anyone to know that Grandad does these things – I'd be so ashamed.' My grandfather was my cousin's rapist. That blew my mind. It confirmed that this thing was really wrong, it shouldn't be happening. Before this, the old man had actually been touching me up and making me do things to him at every opportunity, but

51

because of what Dad was doing to me, it barely registered. I'd never used the word rape for the things that were done to me, but that day, I thought, *this isn't right. I'm being raped too.* Also, the big thing was, this was a woman I thought had the perfect life, a woman whose life *was* perfect. Now I realised, she was just like that, just like me.

Valerie kept pleading with Mum not to tell anyone, and Mum promised not to, but it reinforced what Dad had told me. *Don't tell anyone. It's your fault. You're to blame. You're the guilty one.* If Valerie felt this bad, then that was obviously proof that it was shameful and it was her/my fault.

'When does the old bastard do it?' Mum was asking her. 'When does he get the chance?'

'Everywhere,' wept Valerie. 'When I visit here, I'll phone beforehand to check Mum is around, then, when I turn up, he'll have sent her out to the shops. He'll turn up at mine at all times of the day to catch me alone – I sometimes think that he watches the house to see when I'm there. He's an expert, Maureen. He's been doing it since I was a little girl so he's pretty much worked out every way he can to get at me.'

'I can't fucking believe it,' said Mum.

And with those words, I realised that I had no chance. If she didn't believe another adult, someone she liked and was friends with, why would she believe me if I ever told her?

It made me look at people differently. Who else was going through this? It made me question everything, including the sort of man my grandfather was if he had been doing that too for years. This seemed to be something women just had to bear, it was what they were there for and the abuse itself was everywhere. I was a woman now too, I felt, now that I had started my period, and I was more like my cousin than I had ever expected.

I want you to know that it's OK to cry, Scarlett. It's OK to feel angry and upset. It's OK to feel. You've trained yourself to go to that little cottage in your mind but I know there are times, before you get there, that it all becomes too much. When you're sitting on your bed crying, all I want to do is give you a massive hug. I know, as a child, that's all you want, to be held and to feel loved without anything else, without there being a price to pay. You yearn for it and no one gives it to you, but they will one day, I promise. I know you struggle to smile and find any happiness. Your friends can smile, your friends can laugh, but they don't have daddies like yours, do they? You are starting to realise that not all daddies treat their daughters the way yours treats you, and that hurts. I know that you know things aren't right but you don't know how to stop it. You're just a child and the adults should be keeping you safe – they won't though, they won't. You are seeing that even grown women, women you find incredible, are victims of this too. But they can rise, and so can you. Hold on, hold on Scarlett.

Chapter Four

Dirty

I came in from school one day and could hear immediately that Mum had friends in. I came in the back door, through the kitchen and living room to get upstairs, but she was at me in a flash, with two other women at her side. She had the candles and magazines in her hand and I could just tell they'd all been talking about me.

'Look what I found,' she said, coolly. 'What have you got to say about this, madam?'

My heart dropped. She was loving this and she adored having an audience. I knew it was wrong, everything was wrong, but I didn't know how to stop any of it. To see her standing there with those *things* made me so embarrassed – but maybe it meant that something would happen?

She hadn't asked any questions when she'd found them in my room, but there were other people here now and the fact that she had chosen to tell them perhaps meant that she was going to look into how in the world a girl my age would have such things. I wanted her to ask the right questions though – my heart was beating so much and I was still terrified that I would be one day taken away, as Dad said that all the time.

'Look! Look at these filthy things!' Mum screamed, no longer calm. 'You're a dirty little slut – what do you do with them? Sit up in your room looking at this and sticking a fucking candle up you?' She had her audience right where she wanted them now; there was no need to change what she had said to me before, as these women hadn't heard it. I assumed that she was acting as if she had just found the things, not that she'd already made me feel awful about it all.

'You dirty slag. If I ever find you with these things again, you'll get it.'

That was it. No questions.

I said nothing, looked at the floor, and ran out of the room, feeling utter shame. I can only guess what they all said about when I left, and I'm sure it gave them plenty of gossip material. I was probably the talk of the bingo for weeks.

It was close to this point that Dad started doing more shifts on the overnight trips. He was really popular, everyone loved good old Brian, and Mum was keen on him doing the long journeys as people tended to have collections at the end for the driver, so he was bringing home extra cash. On top of that, Mum just wanted to play happy families with the foster kids, so the more people she could have from out under her feet, the better. Naturally, I loved when he was away, although when he got back, there was always a lot of catching up to do and the abuse seemed to intensify as he tried to make up for lost time.

'Why don't you treat yourself to the bingo tonight, Maureen,' he'd say, splashing the cash. 'Have a couple of sessions, maybe you'll get a full house this time – you feeling lucky, love?' Mum never had to be told twice to get down the bingo hall, and it seemed as if their relationship was on a reasonably even keel. There was never any return to the refuge and, while they weren't exactly Romeo and Juliet, they had a deal. Dad brought in the money and battered two of the three kids, she went to bingo and hit us all. I sometimes wonder what those little twins thought of it all. Even though I'm still in touch with them, it's something we've never discussed. I don't think for a minute that Dad was abusing them, but I do think they must have noticed something as time went on, even if it was just the difference between how Mum treated them as opposed to her biological kids.

'Are you sure you'll be alright with this lot, Brian?' she asked, knowing that he would say he was perfectly capable. 'The twins are no trouble but I wish I could say the same for the other three little shits. I swear to God they've never given me a moment's peace since you left. They'd try the patience of a saint.'

He just wanted rid of her – and I knew why. 'You are a bloody saint, Maureen, proper good Mum you are. You deserve a night off.'

'Well, if you're sure . . .'

Five minutes later, off she went in a haze of Elnett hairspray and her favourite Avon perfume, puffing away at a fag, handbag clasped tightly with the 20 quid in it that Dad had paid her to leave her daughter with him.

'Just you and me now,' he smiled.

'I've got homework to do,' I lied.

'Have you fuck,' he replied. 'I've missed you – now, be a good girl and get upstairs.'

It was all so predictable, and so hideous. He came home, Mum went to bingo, and I went to my imaginary cottage with the waves crashing in the background while he did unspeakable things to me.

On one of the occasions when he got home from a another long trip, Dad told me his next plan. 'Summer holidays soon, Princess. How about you come away with me for a little trip?'

'No,' I said instantly. The thought of a full night with him turned my stomach. 'I wouldn't be allowed,' I told him.

'Who's going to stop it?' he laughed. 'I'm your fucking Dad and I allow it!'

'No – Mum wouldn't like it.'

'Mum couldn't care less, and you know it. You just make out that you want to go, that you need a break from the others, and it'll all be fine. You'll like it, it'll be nice.' He always used those words, those lies. I never liked it, it was never nice, and this wouldn't be any different.

He was right on one thing though. Mum couldn't wait to see the back of me.

'Good fucking riddance,' she said when Dad raised the topic, as he winked at me when she spoke. 'Can you take the whole fucking lot of them, Brian?' She didn't mean the twins, she loved them, but my other two siblings looked at me as if I had landed a prize.

'You need a break, Maureen,' he told her. 'Sooner rather than later. I've got an old folks' trip tomorrow. This one can come along on that. Couple of nights away will do you both good.'

Tomorrow! I thought I would have had some time to prepare myself – not that I ever could – but it was so soon. The less time I had before it happened, the less chance I would have to try and get out of it.

My mind is blank as to how I spent the day before, what I took on the trip, or even where we went. It might have been Lake Windermere but I'm not sure. I sat in the front seat and we did pick-ups of old people before the actual real drive began. I didn't want that part to end and dreaded what would happen that night when we were alone. I had no one to talk to and fear built up inside me all day. I suppose there were some nice parts – I loved the scenery, I remember that, and when we stopped off at cafés or service stations, the old people bought me sweets or magazines. They were all really lovely but when we got back on, I was alone, knowing what was coming to me. We drove through a lot of open space and I wished I could just jump right out of that van and run away forever. Each time we made another stop and one of the OAPs said how lucky I was to have such a nice dad who took me places, I wanted to scream at them. Why didn't I? Why didn't I take the opportunity to tell someone who wasn't linked to my family? Well, I guess I still had that lingering belief that this was all my fault, that I made him act this way; and, if that was the truth, I would be the one who was taken away.

When we got to the final destination, wherever it was, the drop-offs started at the various places people were staying. Everyone was saying goodbye to Dad, saying what a lovely man he was. I knew what he was. They couldn't see it but I knew.

'Right,' Dad said when he'd dropped off the last elderly couple. 'Time for us! I've got a nice little B&B in mind.' It was dark by this point. He parked outside a big house and hopped out of the driver's seat. 'Come on Scarlett – straighten your face. There's nothing to worry about. I've even got us two single beds if that's what you're being miserable about.'

I tried to believe him, but he'd never told me the truth about what was coming to me during any of this, so why would he come through now? The owners obviously knew Dad and seemed delighted to meet his daughter. They couldn't have thought for a minute that there was anything untoward going on – why would that even cross their minds? When we got to the bedroom, I was shocked when I saw that he had told the truth about one thing – there were two single beds! I felt a little bit of relief at that but it soon dissolved.

'Long day,' he yawned. 'Get undressed, Princess. No need for pyjamas.' I did as I was told and slipped under the thin sheet as quickly as possible, even though he was watching me. He didn't say a word at that point, just took his own clothes off and got in beside me. The two beds had just been for show.

It happened again there and then; that was one of the worst experiences for me of them all (which is saying something) as he stayed in the bed all night. He fell asleep without a care in the world while I barely closed my eyes, feeling his disgusting breath on me as he breathed in and out right next to my face for the whole night. He was treating me like a girlfriend, someone to cuddle up to all night when they had sneaked away from prying eyes. How can you get away from an adult man in a single bed? Only in your thoughts. I went to the little cottage in my imagination, dissociating but on guard waiting for it to happen again. Which it did.

When we got up in the morning we headed straight back home – he had no pick-ups on the way back and must have just wanted us to spend the night together. In his mind, it had been a success and he chatted normally on way back as if we'd had a lovely break. He was always happy afterwards and I guess that's why I did it. Any time he got angry with everyone else, it was never at me. I paid my dues with the abuse and he gave me the love Mum could never provide. How sick is that?

At senior school, my behaviour was going downhill fast. I couldn't be bothered. I wanted to pay attention but how can any child do that in school when they've spent all night with their dad coming in and putting his hand up their nightie? He'd appear at the door and check if Jackie and I were both asleep. If she was awake, he'd just say goodnight. If not, he'd be at me. He could do it so quietly that she never woke up – at least I didn't think so. And me? I was always such a good girl that I only kept my hatred of it in my mind, never thinking that if I screamed out, someone would come running. Who would save me? who would actually care? When I was actually at school, I was often exhausted from staying awake from listening out for him or watching the door to see if he would appear. Learning didn't seem nearly as important as that, and there were days when I would fall asleep in class, hating the teachers who would shout at me for 'slacking'. How can a child do homework when they are living in that environment, how can they snuggle up on a chair to read a book? If there are any teachers reading this, that is one of the main things I would want them to take away – when a child plays up, when they disrupt, ask yourself why. I wasn't stupid, but my love for maths and art was long gone. Why would that be, they should have wondered. Where had that child gone?

Mum was loath to spend money on us so when there was a school trip to Germany offered in the second year of senior school, I assumed there was no chance for me to go on it. For some unfathomable reason, the otherwise horrible German teacher liked me – even though I was shocking at it – and she actually paid for me to go! I have wondered about that over the years and considered whether she knew there was something wrong, or 'off' about my home life. It was so out of character for her to be nice, but she didn't take it any further, she didn't ask me any questions. I was hugely grateful though and it was amazing - the freedom of someone not coming in at night for three nights was indescribable.

I had a friend at school who was on the trip too, a girl called Fiona who knew nothing of my home life. Fiona and I wandered round markets, went to the beach, and generally enjoyed the absolute freedom we had. One day, we were sitting on a bench, watching the world go by, when a bloke walking in our direction flashed us. Fiona started screaming and crying whilst I thought, *what an overreaction*.

That was when I really started to think that I was different, that maybe what Dad did to me wasn't what all dads did – if it was, why did Fiona act like she'd never seen one of those before? Wouldn't she have seen her own dad's by now? We went back to the youth hostel and she told the teacher, who called the police. They took statements but I just couldn't see what the drama was. Fiona had obviously never seen one before and that continued to make me think – maybe this wasn't normal for everyone. I had lots of friends but I didn't want a best one as they might suspect something, and this event made me feel I was quite right to do that. I had to act shocked along with Fiona. I didn't want her wondering why I was so nonplussed about what was obviously a shocking thing to her. I couldn't risk her going back and telling everyone else. I couldn't risk them finding out that I was a dirty slag.

That phrase was always in my mind – it was how I saw myself and it was what Mum called me regularly. I was starting to wonder – if, as Dad said, all fathers and daughters did this, why did none of my friends talk about it? If it was normal, then, surely, we couldn't all be dirty slags, and we couldn't all be ashamed of what was happening. Why was it a secret? Why did he tell me it had to stay that way or I was the one who would be blamed and sent from the house? It didn't add up. *Finally*, it didn't add up. The fact that Fiona had made such a big deal out of the flasher had opened my eyes, and it was another piece in the puzzle for me, just as the moment with cousin Valerie had been.

When I got back from Germany, I found out that Jackie had been taken to hospital. Everyone was very vague about it, and wouldn't answer my questions about why she had been taken in. When she returned home after a few days, she wouldn't tell me any details either.

'I'd had enough,' she said, wearily.

'Enough of what? Was it your appendix?' A friend from school had been through a burst appendix that year and it was the only thing I could think of that would make someone go into hospital so quickly.

'I told you – I'd had enough,' Jackie replied, turning to face the wall. She could say what she liked as far as I was concerned. I didn't care about her – why didn't Dad rape her, how did she get away from it? I didn't want to be the good girl any longer, I didn't want to be the only one dealing with this so I started playing up at school even more. Was it to try and get attention, to make someone finally ask the right questions? Probably. I don't really have an answer, but it seemed like the only option.

One day, when Jackie had returned to school and we were both back home, we were sitting on the sofa, watching telly. We never really chatted to each other – she was quite distant and I resented that she wasn't being abused, as horrible as that sounds. Mum was out with the twins and I could hear the water running from Dad being in the shower. As usual, he started banging on the floor.

'You go,' I said to Jackie.

'What the fuck are you talking about?' she answered.

'You go and see what Dad wants.'

'Will I fuck,' she swore at me. 'I'm not going anywhere near that old bastard – you go.'

'No.' I was going to stand my ground.

'Well, it's you or no one,' she told me. 'I'm not spending another minute with him. You're the princess after all, so go see your beloved daddy.'

This was such a strange thing to say. I knew that I was his favourite, but what did Jackie mean about not going 'near' him? She got up from the sofa as the banging continued and walked towards the door.

'Jackie!' I shouted. 'Why? Why don't you want to go?' I paused, knowing that if I said the words I wanted to say, I could never take them back. 'Is it because he does to you what he does to me?' My big sister turned around and looked at me. She never said a word, just held my gaze – then ran out the back door, leaving me to go upstairs.

That night, when Mum came back to the house after bingo, Dad had left for work. Jackie must have said something to her, because as soon as she saw me, she started ranting and raving.

'I've told you before – don't make up shit! Don't tell lies! You dirty fucking slag! Keep your dirty fucking mouth shut!'

What did she know, I wondered? What exactly was it she wanted me to shut up about? There were so many secrets in that house, and I didn't know I had the power to blow so much of it open. There were rumours at school that Jackie had actually tried to kill herself, that she had taken an overdose, but that was never brought up either.

Dad had started making me put my head over the edge of the bed when I was in his room. He'd force me to suck him while he 'performed' oral sex on me. I hate that word.

'Performed'. It sounds like the other person is doing something for the pleasure or benefit of the other, which is a hundred miles away from what I was feeling. I always gagged on it, especially because he would force himself into my mouth at an angle to get his penis further in. I got used to the rape but I never got used to that. I thought it was the worst thing he could ever think of to do. I should have known better.

I was 13 years old when I had the worst moment of my life so far. In their bedroom, there was a stool for them to get into the attic. It was metal frame with a square wooden top, like the sort you get in science classes. One day, Dad called up me up and told me to get undressed. That was my normal. That was my life – but then he told me to bend over the stool.

I had no idea what he was after, but fear washed over me.

'Don't want to,' I told him.

'Just do it. Bend over and shut up.'

'Don't want to.'

'Oh Christ – just fucking do it, Scarlett.'

There was little preamble by that stage. He'd just bark commands at me, without calling me Princess, without telling me I was special. I refused another few times, but he was getting angrier and angrier at me, so I did it. I put my arms over the side and bent across the wooden top of the stool. I assumed that he was going to hit me or rape me from the position behind me, but he didn't. He didn't do it in the 'usual' place. I hadn't even known such a thing existed but the pain was like nothing I had ever imagined. I screamed as soon as he started, as soon as I knew where he was trying to put it, trying to scramble off the stool in desperation, but he kept pushing me back, pushing, pushing. He didn't care.

That is my worst memory. The pain was so intense that I lost that day and myself completely. Before that act, I could emotionally remove myself from the rapes, but now I was removed from everything. I had been screaming for him to get off me, to leave me alone because it hurt so much, but he couldn't have cared less. He had an empty house and he had a victim who was so tied up in what he was doing that she would tell no one.

A part of me gave up that day.

There is such a lesson I want you to learn here Scarlett, because it is one that all victims and survivors struggle with – just because there are moments that are fine, doesn't mean that the rest of it wasn't Hell. When you were on that trip, it was nice to get away and it was nice to spend time with the old people treating you well. But you weren't being punished for that by what he did to you. There isn't an invisible set of scales. Just because you had a good day otherwise didn't make what he did to you OK. When it happens, I want you to stay in your happy place, go to that lovely cottage by the sea and listen to the waves. I know that, inside, you are dying right now so you do what you need to do to survive and get through it, but please keep telling yourself it was not your fault. Little Scarlett, I see you in my mind's eye so clearly even after all these years. You will get through it, you must, because I'm here now, telling our story, but I do have these things to tell you and I hope that in doing so, I can speak not just to the me from so long ago but to anyone who is going through or has gone through this. There are so many of us, too many to count, but we're an army, and one day, like you, we will rise.

Chapter Five

Pretty

After that day, I wanted to die. It took away any sense that I could deal with it, that I could deal with the horrors of my life. I didn't want any of this for a second longer. Every time I went to bed, I didn't want to wake up. I wondered whether the rumours were true and that Jackie had tried to kill herself. If she had, how had she done it, and, more importantly, what had she got wrong that she was still here?

I was bored at school and I was disruptive. I was quick and clever, so I finished work in five minutes and then disrupted the class for the rest of the period. They moved me down a class for everything as punishment but all that achieved was giving me the chance to finish work quicker as it was easier – which left me more time to be more disruptive. Teachers all told me I'd amount to nothing and I believed them. It all seemed a waste of time.

One day, we were in biology and there was a specific sex education class. It was all very twee. There was a film about the practical side, what men and women have on their bodies, about where everything goes, about cells and conception. There was talk of them loving each other and the special things they would do. It was all nonsense.

'What a crock of shit,' I said, loudly.

'Scarlett Jones!' shouted the biology teacher. 'Some of us would like to watch this, please. I suggest you do too, you might learn something.'

'Crock of fucking shit,' I said again.

'Would you like to enlighten us?' he asked. 'Would you like to tell us all what a girl like yourself knows so much better than the combined resources and knowledge of an entire scientific base of knowledge?'

'It's fuck all to do with the science,' I shouted at him. 'You can stick whatever dick in whatever hole you like. But all this crap about love and special feelings? I think you are completely deluded if you believe that's what happens.'

Naturally, I got thrown out of class but, again, why did no one ask why I knew these things or why I was so angry about it all?

By the time I was about 14, Dad had started doing some long-distance trips abroad. He could be away for two or three weeks at a time, which did mean that I got some respite, but once he got back, it was every day. He was obsessed and possessed. As soon as he could, he'd be at me. If he got back at night-time, he would creep into my room. If he got back during the day, he'd pray that Mum was at bingo and he could distract Jackie (not that she was often at home and Joey had left by now). He always found a way, starting by groping me if there were people around, putting his hand up my school skirt and touching my breasts, all working up to when he could get me alone.

Mum was fostering again. The twins had left after a year or so, but there was a family nearby who had two little boys in need of fostering. When their plans fell through, Mum was asked if she could step in. Philip was about eight, and Mark was five or so. They were gorgeous kids but they had serious issues. Mark was constantly touching himself. I didn't know if he had done it before he came to us, or whether it was new behaviour, so my mind automatically went to Dad. Was he abusing this little boy as well? Often when Mark touched himself, he would do it in front of us all which seemed peculiar, as if he didn't actually know it was wrong. Had someone made him think it was normal?

'Look at me, look at me, look at me!' he would say.

Dad never did. Mum would tell him to stop, but he never looked at him at all, never made eye contact. Eventually, it got so bad that Mum had to tell the social worker who was in charge of their case.

He came out, sat on the sofa and listened to everything Mum told him. Mark was playing on the floor during the meeting and didn't do a single one of the things Mum had described.

'It's normal,' said the social worker. 'Perfectly normal.'

'You don't see it,' said Mum. 'No way is that normal.'

'It's really important that you don't make Mark feel he is doing anything wrong,' he continued. 'Children need to discover their own bodies. Really, it's completely normal.'

I was sitting there thinking, *ask me, please ask me what is normal in this house.* To be honest, I resented that Mum had rung social workers about Mark but not me. Maybe if she didn't have them, she'd have noticed me as I was unravelling. They were royalty to her, I was nothing. I was a skivvy to her – *wash the dishes, tidy up, get the hoover out, dust for fuck's sake, why do I have to do everything?* She did nothing unless it was with or for Mark and Philip, but she had a slave for the housework in me. The foster kids and bingo, that was all she cared about. I know that I should have done more to make sure they were fine, especially Mark, and I still feel guilty about that, but I was barely hanging on myself. I also thought that, given Mum adored them, she would keep them safe in a way she had never managed for me.

My life now consisted of being an outsider at school, then coming home and being treated like an outsider there. I started staying out as late as I could rather than going home. Dad was bringing crates of Cinzano back from duty free after his work trips abroad and I'd steal them regularly, necking whole bottles at a time. I'd discovered the glorious state of drunkenness – when I was drunk, I didn't need to think. My best friend at that stage was a girl called Louise. She was from a perfect family, with lovely parents, but like me she wasn't part of any group. We were both on the outside looking in, so it was almost a foregone conclusion that we would be drawn to each other. We'd get drunk together on the bottles I'd managed to steal and hang around the streets or the school playground when it was closed, just being teenagers.

I had started to get home later and later from school or from my sessions with Louise, dreading going back if Dad wasn't away but also hating being there if it was just Mum being obsessed with those bloody kids. The feeling of resentment had built up even more since the visit from the social worker, and I hated the fact that she noticed them so quickly when she had never noticed me for years. She was obviously capable of being caring and loving, so why hadn't she managed it with us? There must have been something very wrong with me, Jackie and Joey for her to hate us and hit us the way she did, whereas these children were good ones that she never even raised her voice to.

I tried to delay home time by going to Lou's house or, as I said, wandering around with her, but on one particular late afternoon, I was on my own. Still in my school uniform, I walked through Regent Street, working out whether I should stay out for even longer. Regent Street was a residential area where all of the Muslims in Telford were put when they moved into the area. There were very few white people there and it could be quite intimidating walking past the gangs of young boys and men who would have eyes on sticks when any white girl walked past. It didn't bother me. They never said anything. I was in a world of my own when this Pakistani lad I had never seen before walked up to me.

'Hi.'

'Erm, hi,' I replied. He didn't look like anyone I knew from school, in fact he looked quite a bit older than me, but I didn't pay much attention to boys so perhaps I had seen him around. 'Do I know you?'

He laughed – he had really white, perfect teeth and was very good-looking. He had a mullet with the long bit at the back permed, but that was pretty fashionable back then, not the crime against hair it is now! 'Not really, but I've seen you around. I've seen you around a lot actually.'

'At school?' I asked.

'No, no!' he was laughing at the idea of that. 'I'm a bit older than you. What age are you anyway? 15?'

'14,' I corrected him but regretted it immediately. I was really flattered that he was talking to me, and now I'd let him know I was a kid.

'Fourteen? Well, you're really pretty – do you know that? I bet you do. I bet you get told that all the time.'

I shrugged casually, thinking *no, no one tells me I'm pretty, they tell me I'm a slag or a waste of space or a dirty slut, but never pretty. They tell me it's my fault they rape me, they tell me that I'll be taken away if I tell anyone, but pretty? No, never pretty.*

'What's your name?'

'Scarlett.'

He smiled. 'Pretty name for a pretty girl, right? I'm Ed – well, that's what my mates call me. So . . . I guess that's what you'll call me too Scarlett, yeah?'

He was charming and I liked that he wasn't from our school. He had no preconceptions of me *and* he thought I was pretty. Today had taken a turn for the better!

'This probably sounds really daft,' he went on, 'but I've got a mate who really fancies you. I mean *really really really* fancies you.' He rolled his eyes and made love heart signs as he was telling me, and I couldn't help but laugh. Ed seemed alright so far – for a lad.

'That's nice,' I replied. 'Does he hang around street corners chatting to schoolgirls he doesn't know too?'

'Oooh, that hurts,' Ed said, pretending that I'd stuck a dagger in his chest. 'Actually, he noticed you a few weeks ago but neither of us could pluck up the courage to chat.'

I couldn't believe that for a second. Who would need to pluck up the courage to speak to me? 'What age are you?'

'19.'

'And your imaginary mate?'

'Swear he's real, swear he is! He's 19 too. Is that OK?'

'OK for what?' I asked, trying to sound casual, but feeling blinded by this boy's smile and his casual way of speaking to me, as if I was human, as if I mattered. 'What is he after?' I was always suspicious.

'He just wondered if you would meet him. See if you get on. See if you're the girl of his dreams like he seems to think. Scarlett – lovely, lovely Scarlett,' he crooned, winking at me.

'Maybe . . .' I ventured, carefully.

'There's a slight problem. He's not actually here just now,' Ed told me. 'He's gone back to Pakistan for a bit, just family stuff, but why don't you meet me later, say 8pm? I'll give you his phone number and you can chat, see if you get on?'

There couldn't be any harm in that, I reckoned. Actually, it was even better if I didn't have to meet him just now, there was no commitment if he was an absolute nightmare. 'OK,' I confirmed. 'Where?'

'Phone box just at the end of the street,' said Ed. 'Eight o'clock, right? Don't forget, pretty girl!'

Every time I looked back, he was waving at me. I really hoped his friend was as nice as him – I wished I'd asked for the other lad's name, but I could do that when I was given his number in a few hours.

As I walked home for tea, I smiled to myself the whole way. I never let boys close to me, but Ed wasn't at school, he didn't live that near to our house, and he wouldn't have heard of my reputation as a troublemaker. It was nice to think that someone, his friend, had a crush on me and it seemed normal – I craved normality and was drawn to it, whether Lou's family or, now, this friend of Ed's. I finished my tea as quickly as I could then rushed upstairs to change. He knew my age but if he saw me again in school uniform, it would make him even more aware of how young I was. I pulled on a pair of jeans and a striped top, took my hair out of its messy ponytail, and covered myself with a liberal dose of Impulse. I wondered if I should put on some of my favourite Rimmel Heather Shimmer lipstick – the one I'd nicked from the local Boots – but I finally decided against it. Maybe it would make me look tarty and that was the last image I wanted to portray. No, jeans and smelling nice, that was all I needed.

By the time I got to the phone box in Regent Street, Ed was already there. I sort of feel like I need to explain some of the things I'm talking about as they're practically history now, but phone boxes were all over the place back then. They didn't just act as somewhere to call someone, they were meeting places for teenagers, snogging and feeling-up boxes really. This one was empty but it was coming up to the time of night where other girls and boys my age would be congregating there, deciding who they'd cop a feel from that night, then going off home to dream of their new love. I could only imagine such things. Ed looked even more like a grown up now, in his cream chinos and smart shirt, and I was delighted – he wasn't one of the stupid, immature lads from school who could think of nothing more delightful to shout than 'show us your tits!' a hundred times a day. I felt really flattered that

Ed was spending any time in my company at all. I kind of wished that someone I knew would see us, not just Lou as I would tell her all about Ed and his friend tomorrow, but one of the other girls, the stuck-up ones who thought they were better than me.

'Hey!' he said as soon as he saw me. 'You came!'

'Yeah, well, nothing else to do,' I shrugged casually.

'You look great, but you looked great in your school uniform too. I bet you'd look gorgeous no matter what you wore, Scarlett. I told my friend that you would talk to him,' Ed told me, 'and he's really keen. Do you still want his number?'

'S'pose so.' I tried to appear so nonchalant, but inside I was yelling, *yes, the phone number, the phone number of your mate who I can only dream is as handsome and lovely as you!*

'OK – if you come with me to my house, I've got it there. You'll have to walk behind me though. My family is really strict and I can't be seen with you. They'd hate me to be friends with a white girl.'

It honestly never crossed my mind that I was meant to be meeting Ed there to get the phone number in the first place but that he had turned up without it. Despite everything, I was actually woefully naïve at times. I just did as he asked, dutifully walking quite a few steps behind him as if we weren't together. It wasn't long before he rounded the corner into a row of terraced houses, going to the front door of a shabby-looking place. The garden was overgrown and there didn't seem to be curtains at most of the windows. He waited until I got there and then slapped his hand to his forehead.

'What an idiot – I've forgotten my key!' he said.

'Is there no one else in?' I asked. It might have been a cliché, but all of the Pakistani families I knew who lived there had big families. As an adult, the alarm bells are ringing, but as a teenage girl, I was pretty immature despite everything I had been through.

'Nah, it's fine. We can climb in the side window,' he explained. It looked normal enough from outside, if a bit tattered, but when I dropped through into the living room after him, there was nothing but a double mattress. That's all there was in the whole room, nothing else but the mattress.

Ed flopped onto it as if he was exhausted. The floor around it was filthy and clearly hadn't been swept, never mind washed, in weeks if not months. The air smelled musty with a lingering smell of cigarette smoke. There were no signs of anyone living there at all, no furniture or ornaments, no pictures in frames or curtains at the windows. There weren't even any lightshades, just bare bulbs, although I doubt there was any electricity anyway. And do you know what I thought? *That's fine, I'm sure there's an explanation for it – maybe someone is just getting ready to move in?*

'What a day!' he said. 'I haven't had a minute to myself. Come here, sit down beside me for a minute, Scarlett.' We just chatted for a bit as I sat beside him on the dirty, stained mattress, he asked me about school, what I was good at, all that sort of thing. He knew the times I had walked down that street before, and he also knew where I lived. I'd been wearing my tie that afternoon, so he must have worked out which school I went to from that, but it was a bit odd that he knew which part of town I lived in. It was nice really. He was the first person I could remember in a long time who was giving me attention even though he didn't have to.

After about 10 minutes, I asked him for his friend's phone number.

'What?' he said, looking surprised.

'Your friend. The one who likes me – the one who has gone back to Pakistan for a bit?'

'Oh yeah . . . him. Well, I'm sure I have it somewhere, but you know, I'm not sure you're his type anyway.'

I felt a drop in my stomach. 'Why not? It was you who said he was keen.'

'I know – but, think about it. You're lying here on a mattress with some guy who is five years older than you who you barely know. I met you three hours ago, Scarlett. You know what they say about white girls . . . and you're kind of keeping that reputation going, aren't you?'

I looked at him in shock. 'Why are you saying such nasty things? I thought you liked me, you said I was pretty, you said both you and your friend thought I was pretty!'

'Oh, you are, you are – absolute stunner,' he replied vaguely. 'Just thinking about it though, my friend . . .' I noticed that Ed had never given this 'friend' a name yet. 'My friend is kind of traditional. He liked looking at you in the shop window but he wouldn't be allowed in to buy, if you know what I mean?'

I wasn't sure I did. I would have been happy with holding hands with this friend of his. I would have even liked waiting for him to come back from Pakistan as that would mean I could just think about him all the time.

'Are you sure you're interested in him anyway, Scarlett? Maybe your attentions are somewhere else,' he teased.

'Have you actually got his phone number?' I asked

'I've got lots of phone numbers,' he laughed. 'Want some? I might give you a few one day. Listen Scarlett, I think we both know what's going on here, don't we? You're maybe only 14 – and I'm kind of glad you are – but you've got plenty going on that someone like me would be interested in. Very interested in.' Ed winked again. God, he really was handsome, and if the friend didn't exist, maybe he had just made him up because he was too shy to ask me out himself? It's amazing the lies you can tell yourself, isn't it?

With that, he pushed me back on the mattress. 'We both know what you're here for, don't we? I certainly know what I have in mind.'

Ed pulled my jeans off and forced himself on me there and then, no more chat, no more friendliness. And all I thought was, *here we go again*. I wasn't even that bothered by it. I thought it was normal, not rape, it was what I was put on this earth for so why would I be surprised? In fact,

I was only really surprised that he had bothered to be nice to me in the first place. He was quick and there was no condom. After he finished, I got up and pulled my jeans on. By the time I was finished, he was already climbing out of the window.

'Ed,' I cried.

He looked round at me, still sitting pathetically on the filthy mattress.

'What?'

'Do you have your friend's number? Please? I think I would like to chat to him after all.'

He looked up at the ceiling and sighed dramatically before saying, 'oh yeah, probably, somewhere – next time?' I climbed out behind him. 'I'll see you soon,' he said when we were both out of the house. It was a statement, not a question, and I could only nod in agreement before he headed off, up Regent Street.

I went home and, honestly, it didn't play on my mind. I didn't want it but it was what I was there for; it seemed to me that women were there to have that done to them. The fact was, Ed had made such an effort to talk to me and to meet up with me despite him running the risk of other Pakistani people being furious if they had seen us together. Maybe it was all a front, maybe he just couldn't help himself, just like Dad. I pushed his lack of interest at the end out of my mind. He had actually been very genuine, I reasoned. He didn't mind that I was younger, that I was white. He was just a man after all, and men did that when they were pushed out of control by looking at women and girls. That's what Dad had told me, and that's what I could see all around me with the girls and boys at school. What had happened to Valerie was wrong, and it shouldn't have happened to me when I was so little, but I was practically grown up and I had found a man who loved me.

He definitely did or he wouldn't have made the effort or taken such risks. I think he would maybe be the one to love me.

I loved him already, I decided. I loved Ed.

Well, this is it, Scarlett, isn't it? I know you feel right now that you have met a genuine person at last. The boy who is the love of your life, who will be there for you despite what he is doing already.

You've listened to everything he says because he is giving you the words you've wanted to hear your entire life . . . please don't trust him. Don't give him your heart – he isn't what you think he is. He isn't going to save you, he's going to continue to abuse you and he's going to taint your view of men for many years to come. Love isn't about rape even though that is all you have known for six years. Love isn't about making the other person feel small or hiding her in the back seat of a car and making her have sex on a filthy mattress on a filthy floor. Love is so far from this. He's just another one who sees you as someone he can use. You've had enough of that, you've had too much of it. Run, Scarlett, run.

Chapter Six

Nothing to worry about

I didn't hear from or see Ed for about a week. There were no mobile phones or social media back in the early 1980s so I couldn't just message or WhatsApp him, all I could do was wonder if he would make an effort to get in touch given that he clearly knew where I lived. I was in love – or so I had convinced myself – and all I knew was that I was waiting for him to tell me again how pretty and special I was. The rape? I wasn't even thinking of it as that. We'd had sex, and that was fine. It wasn't as if I was a virgin. He was pretty much a grown man, and I couldn't expect him to do much else. Love made it OK anyway and I suspected this was just the start of a perfect relationship.

I walked down Regent Street a few times to try and see Ed, running the gauntlet of disapproving looks from Pakistani boys and men, but there was no sign of him. They had started to shout out 'white slag' and other names but I think I was maybe just hearing them for the first time. At school, the girls all spoke about how they were called that if they ever went that route, which meant that I didn't automatically think Ed had said anything to them if some were his friends. It was just something that happened in that area, and it was water off a duck's back. The fact that he had raped me wasn't a huge consideration about how I thought of him – as I've said before, the whole concept of 'rape' wasn't one that I often applied to what was done to me over the years. When I'd heard cousin Valerie confiding in Mum that Christmas, yes, that had hit home, but as time had passed, it became something that I just thought I was there for. Ed had been nice to me really, and I held onto that, not letting my mind wander to anything else. He had just done what men do to women, no more, no less. I did tell Lou some of it, but not those parts.

'What? You've got a boyfriend?' she screeched. 'All of a sudden, you've got a BOYFRIEND? God, Scarlett

– you kept that quiet. What's he like, what's he like? Tell me everything.'

'Well, he's 19 . . .'

'19! God, you lucky bitch – bet he knows how to treat you right, not like these idiots here,' she rolled her eyes at the boys in the playground.

'Oh, he's lovely Louise, always telling me how pretty I am. He says that all his mates fancy me and that he's the lucky one.' Nothing wrong with a bit of embellishment, I thought, and, anyway, he had *almost* said that.

'How long have you been seeing him? Where does he take you? Have you been on nights out?' Louise wanted to know everything.

'I've been seeing him quite a while,' I lied, although it had been a week since the filthy mattress, and I thought that counted *as* a week, 'and yeah, we've been out.' From the phone box to the dirty mattress. I just needed a narrative of love. I needed to make someone else believe it all and then I would be able to believe it too.

Louise sighed a lot. 'I wish I had that. You're just so lucky, Scarlett.'

A week later, I came out of school and Ed was finally there, beeping his car outside school gates. He had remembered me, he did want me! Maybe I hadn't imagined it after all.

'Who's that? Who's that?' I was asked by about a dozen other girls at once.

I looked at Louise and whispered, 'that's him – that's Ed.'

She stared back at me, open-mouthed. 'He's gorgeous, Scarlett – you lucky, lucky bitch!'

As I looked at him in bright daylight, I could see that he wasn't exactly gorgeous but he was good-looking enough, especially compared to what we were used to with the annoying, spotty, smelly boys at school. I was the centre of attention as he sat leaning out of the open window of his gleaming red car, clearly a man rather than the annoying hordes of lads piling out of the school gates.

'Hey Scarlett!' he called.

I was really proud when he shouted my name, thankful for the scrap of recognition that he'd even remembered it. I walked straight to his car, casually shouting back to the other girls who had been asking friends, 'just off to see my boyfriend now!'

They all stood watching as I went over.

'Hiya!' I brightly said. 'It's soooo nice to see you!' I bent over to the window hoping for a kiss in front of everyone, but he was brusque.

'Yeah, yeah, you too. Get in, will you?' He was perfectly nice, but a bit abrupt. I walked round the other side, but he hissed, 'in the back, in the back, remember I can't be seen with you!' That was fine by me and I went there, hoping none of the girls watching would question why I was doing it. I knew that Pakistani boys were encouraged – sometimes forced – to only be with girls from their own culture, and I felt it added a little bit of danger to our relationship. It would be a forbidden love, and all the more exciting for that.

'No! Lie down,' Ed snapped at me as I started to put my seat belt on. 'For fuck's sake, Scarlett, I really can't have anyone see that you're here.'

'I'm sorry, I'm sorry!' I did as I was told – I pretty much always did as I was told – and lay on the back seat as he drove off. I was still in my uniform and a bit worried that my skirt would ride up as I lay there, so I kept pulling it down self-consciously. That sticks in my mind. He'd already raped me, he'd already ripped jeans off me and had sex with me on a filthy mattress in a deserted house, but I was concerned that he might see my knickers in the car.

'Stop fidgeting,' Ed said. 'What the fuck are you doing back there?'

'Keeping myself decent!' I answered.

He looked at me in the rearview mirror. 'Don't worry about that, I like your uniform, I like it all – and anyway, we've nothing to hide, have we?'

I smiled back at him. *We*. That was all it took to convince me that we were a couple after all. As he drove, Ed did chat to me, nothing important, just asking about my day, did I like school, that sort of thing. 'Fancy going up the Wrekin?' he asked. The Wrekin is a hill to the west of Telford, and a popular place for walkers, probably hundreds of them go there every day, with a café halfway for them to rest. I knew that it was also a popular place for couples to go, as there are loads of places for cars to park.

'Sure,' I replied. 'Sure.' I hoped for a bit of kissing, a bit of romance, before we'd both have to drive back and part, broken-hearted. I didn't fancy a walk, but if he wanted to do that, I wouldn't complain.

Not quite, Scarlett, not quite.

The main car park is big, dark, under lots of trees, and, as soon as he had put the handbrake on, Ed climbed in the back with me. 'Oh, hi you,' I said, so pleased that he was making an effort, but there was no chit-chat and definitely no romance. Pushing my school skirt up and ripping my knickers off, there was clearly only one thing on his mind.

'Are we going for a walk?' I asked him. 'Do you want to get some fresh air?'

'Sssh, sssh,' he hissed, just as Dad did when he wanted to shut me up.

'I really like you, Ed,' I told him. 'Do you like me? I think we could be so good together, don't you?'

There was no answer; instead, as usual, all I got was a man sticking his dick into me as quickly as he could. He had sex for him, there was nothing for me, then he rushed back to the driver's seat.

'Back to school?' he asked, as if nothing had happened.

'Yeah, sure,' I said, a bit stunned by how little he had even bothered to talk to me once he got in the back of the car. I scrambled to get my knickers from the floor as he hissed for me to keep lying down, but that was OK – he was definitely my boyfriend now as we'd done it twice, and I knew he would be restricted with dating a white girl. I should just be glad that I'd made him happy really. Before I knew it, he was dropping me off at the school gates.

'Bye Ed!' I called, hopefully, but he didn't even look back and certainly didn't say if or when I would see him again. We had been gone 45 minutes at the most.

School was closed with just a few cars there belonging to teachers or cleaners or janitors who were still working. There were a few lads playing football in the playground and it all seemed so normal, so plain and boring. I was stunned by how quickly everything had happened but I focused on the fact that I had a boyfriend, an older man who clearly adored me as he was willing to run the risk of being ostracised by his family to be with me. I was a fool. A fool who had known nothing else since she was a child of eight, but a fool nonetheless. I feel as though there are certain moments in your life when someone comes into it or something happens that should have a flag flying and sirens blazing, telling you that this matters so much. If only that were the case.

I had no idea that day that the Wrekin would become a symbol of my exploitation, that it wouldn't be somewhere beautiful I could escape to, it would just be a place for hideous things to be done to my battered body. I also didn't know that I wasn't the only one and that the same place would become a mark for the abuse of so many young girls for the next 30 years and more. It is sad to think of how such a stunning spot has been tainted, but what I didn't know was that the Wrekin was a recognised spot for men like Ed to take girls like me.

Ed turning up at the school gates became a regular occurrence. He'd be waiting for me two or three times a week and the others just accepted that he was my boyfriend now. He'd always take me back to the Wrekin, back to the same secluded spot in the car park, and it would all happen again. He stopped chatting quite quickly really, he never asked anything about me, there was no interest in me as a person at all. I'd convinced myself not to care. I was in love and I had no concept of normality.

I was now suffering the same fate with two men, even if I had convinced myself that Ed was different. Dad was still raping me whenever he was at home, but using condoms, whereas Ed never wore them at all. It wasn't long after I turned 15 that I realised I hadn't had a period for quite some time. There was no reason to think it was for any reason other than the obvious as I'd always been regular. Christ, no. Not that. I was terrified but didn't want to think about it. I didn't want a baby. I *definitely* didn't want a baby. What would Ed think of me? He'd think I had trapped him and he might even wonder if it was his. He was the only one I was having sex with in my mind – Dad was doing the same thing, but I had that in another category and it couldn't be him because of the condoms. No, if I was pregnant, it could only be Ed's, and I couldn't risk losing him.

I lifted drawers. Shifted wardrobes. Carried things about the house that didn't need carrying.

'You cleaning again?' Mum would ask. 'Christ, I've had to beg you for fucking years to even lift a duster and now you're scrubbing floors and climbing ladders for fucking cobwebs as if it's a new hobby.'

Nothing worked. I just knew I was pregnant and, soon, I could see my belly starting to swell. I felt sick in the mornings and there were so many smells that I just couldn't bear. I held cardigans round me all the time, I avoided anyone seeing me when I changed for PE. When I had missed four periods, I finally bought a test. Back then, the tests came with little bottles that you did a wee in, and a stick which came up with lines or not, depending on whether it was negative or positive. I took everything out of the box, read the instructions and put the bottle and the stick under different piles of clothes in my bedroom drawers. If someone did find them, at least they wouldn't be in a container screaming PREGNANCY TEST. I should have known Mum wouldn't have stopped snooping after the horror of the candles and the magazines, and it was only the next day that she started screaming at me.

'What the fuck is this?' she yelled, holding the bottle in my face. 'You're on fucking drugs, aren't you?'

I had no idea where she'd got that from, or why she would think a tiny little bottle was some sort of drugs paraphernalia. I guess if I had left it all in the box, she would have known, but that was the very reason I had taken it all out in separate bits. I wanted anyone who found it to be confused or ignore it, but I didn't know she would decide it was something to do with a bizarre drugs ritual! Naturally, I denied it all – which was easy to do – but, yet again, Mum had missed the chance to ask me the right questions. A caring mother would have at least asked what it was all about rather than give up once she'd thrown wrong conclusions her daughter's way, but mine just wandered off swearing after throwing the plastic bottle at me.

'You're a fucking disgrace,' she muttered. 'An absolute embarrassment to me. What if anyone else had found it? What would have happened then? They could have died Scarlett, they could have died.' I knew she meant danger to kids other than me, but I was bemused by the fact that she had me down as pretty much a heroin addict rather than someone who had a little bottle hidden in their room. It wasn't as if she'd found a stack of used needles lying around the place.

I had to tell Ed. It was clear that I wasn't going to be able to bring on a miscarriage. I didn't know what was going to happen and still didn't really face up to the fact that this could all end in an actual baby. There must have been some element of fear as I just couldn't tell him to his face. I decided to write him a letter. In the middle of the night, I held a torch under the covers as I tried to get the words out. In the end, all I could manage was:

I'm pregnant.

I'm so sorry.

I don't know what to do.

Please help me.

The next morning, I had a change of mind. I had planned to put it in my pocket to give him after school the next time I saw him, hopefully that day, but it seemed a huge undertaking. I decided that, if he did turn up, I would be brave. Maybe he would take me in his arms and tell me it was what he wanted? We could move away if his family threw him out, we could start afresh somewhere else. I thought about it all day, and probably didn't disrupt classes as much as usual. All I wanted was the bell to ring – but, when it did, there was no sign of Ed. I waited for about an hour, kidding myself that he would soon be there, before giving up and going home. I even went back along Regent Street, but there was no sign of him. As usual, I was faced with an onslaught of insults.

'Slag!'

'White trash!'

'Filthy slut!'

The Pakistani boys from the area were sitting on walls outside the houses mostly, and they'd had plenty of time to get home from school as I'd dawdled along hoping to see Ed. The difference this time was that I thought they were probably right. Everything that had gone before was just what I thought I deserved – this, this pregnancy at 15, was a situation that a real slut would find herself in. My emotions were all over the place. I blamed myself, not Ed. I should have done something, I should have prevented it. I couldn't even blame it on Dad. It would have been horrific to be carrying his child, but he had been careful ever since my first period. He had been questioning me for a while as to whether I had a boyfriend, but I always denied it.

'I bet you do, I bet you do. Girl like you – bet they're lining up for you. And it isn't as if you don't know what to do, is it? I've taught you well, I've been a good Dad to you,' he'd leer.

When I got home, after finally accepting I wouldn't be able to track down Ed, Dad was waiting for me. Holding the letter. Honestly, I thought I would collapse with fear, with absolute terror. That was one fucked up day. I expected him to go mental, but instead he walked towards me and gave me a hug.

'Don't worry about it, don't worry about it at all,' he said, warmly. 'These things happen, Princess. Go upstairs and have a lie down, then we can talk about it. Mum's at bingo, the others are all out, even the little ones are at a friend's house for tea. Your old man will be there for you, we'll work this out, don't you worry.'

I couldn't believe it. I had been braced for an absolute attack of name calling and verbal abuse, but he was actually acting like a real dad. There was such a sense of relief – maybe now, finally, someone would be there for me.

I should have known better.

He walked into my room just a few minutes after I lay down on the bed, taking his clothes off as he walked towards me. 'You know, Scarlett? There's one good thing to come out of this? I don't have to use protection any more. Better for both of us. Do you remember how it used to be at the start? Didn't have to worry about it back then. It's not very nice for the man you know, it doesn't feel the same, and I bet it was nicer for you too.'

That's why he had been so laidback. It was all about him. He'd often complained about how it wasn't the same with one, I now recalled, and now he could just do what he wanted. What a shame for him – he had been fine when he could rape an eight, nine, 10-year-old little girl without something spoiling his pleasure, but as soon as I'd got my period he'd been really hard done by, hadn't he? Something clicked inside me that afternoon and I realised that I didn't want him anywhere near me for a second longer.

'No,' I said, for the first time in a while. 'Fuck off, Dad. I don't want this. I don't want it. I hate it, I hate it so much.' I had a baby now. Inside me was a child and I didn't want him, I didn't want *that*, near my baby. It wasn't right.

'Don't be stupid, Princess,' he told me. 'It'll be fine.' Even if I had been the one trying to get rid of it, that was my choice and I wanted to be able to choose now to stop this bastard from sticking his dick anywhere near me or my child.

I couldn't remember the last time he had called me 'Princess' but it would be the last time. He had to force me that day but I made a vow while he was on top of me, grunting and panting, that it would never happen again. And it didn't.

I fell asleep, exhausted by the bone-crushing fatigue of early pregnancy, and when I woke for school, my first thought was that I had to tell Ed. When I had vowed never to let Dad rape me again, never to stick that anywhere near me and my baby, there had been that change in me. I wanted this little one now. I had automatically thought of 'my baby' when he came close to me, and that meant something.

I told Mum that morning as I ran out to school and, all day, again, prayed that Ed would be there when I left. Again, there was no sign of him. What was going on? Why wasn't he wanting to see me? Another walk along Regent Street, another barrage of insults, knowing what was waiting for me when I got home. Mum hated me at the best of times but shouting *I'm pregnant!* at her as I ran out that morning was something that I knew would unleash appalling abuse from her.

However, as it had been with Dad initially, she surprised me.

'I've booked you an appointment with the GP,' she said, quite calmly. 'We'll get you sorted.'

'What? You're not mad?

'Mad? Why would I be mad?' she asked, quizzically.

'You do know I'm pregnant? You do know that's what I said to you this morning?'

'I'm not fucking stupid, Scarlett,' she said, returning to type momentarily. 'I've got a pile of fucking kids. I know what pregnant means.'

'And that's fine? You're fine with that?'

'Of course I am – you know I love children.'

Well, she did love the foster kids, but she couldn't stand any of her biological ones. Maybe this would be different because it was mine, maybe it was just being an actual Mum she couldn't bear.

'OK,' I said, cautiously. 'OK – maybe it'll work.'

'Why wouldn't it work? I'll adopt it. You can get on with your life and I'll be a mum again.'

Christ.

She wanted to take my baby from me.

You've let him in your life now, Scarlett, and there were no flags, no warning sirens – but it's done. You don't know how much he will colour your life or what he has planned for you, but it's done. You have so many of them to contend with but keep an eye on your mother, don't underestimate her for a second. You've seen how duplicitous she is – with the twins, with other people. She can make herself be anything she wants to be and she'll make herself the perfect candidate to take on your baby. She isn't offering to help, is she? She's offering to take away the most precious thing you will ever have. They're coming at you from all sides but don't for a second think that it's because you're weak. What they do will be something for their conscience to bear, and one day they will face judgement – not now, but sometime. They will be seen for what they are and you will be seen for what you are. A survivor. Look after that little one and watch them all, watch them all for there isn't a single one of them who cares for you.

Chapter Seven

You belong to me

To my utter relief, I saw Ed the next day. I needed him more than ever. Home life was going to get even more unbearable. I'd said 'no' to Dad and promised myself he would never do those things to me again, and I had Mum determined to take my baby. He had to be on my side, and I held onto my dream of the three of us making a new life for ourselves away from this place. I hated Telford, I hated everything that was associated with it.

I got into the front passenger seat and he looked at me as if I was mad. 'What the fuck are you doing, are you braindead? Get in the back and lie down!'

'No, Ed, I don't want to go to the Wrekin today,' I bravely told him. 'I want to chat.'

'You want to chat?' he parroted back. 'You want to chat? About what, Scarlett? About dollies and playing? About puppies and unicorns?' I could feel the tears springing to my eyes. Why was he being so mean? I wasn't a kid, I was his girlfriend. 'I don't have time to chat, I've only got time to fuck you – and you should be grateful, so do as I say and get in the back of this car!'

I climbed over, still a good girl, but when I got there, said, 'I still want to talk to you, Ed.'

'Well, I don't want to talk to you.' He put his music on, some awful Pakistani chanting stuff that I hated. I knew I had to tell him, it would never be easy, but it was the first step towards our new life.

'Ed – I have news. Really good news.' I could see him looking at me in the mirror but he didn't react. 'Ed – I'm pregnant, we're going to have a baby.' He started shouting at me immediately, as soon as I got the words out.

'You are kidding me? You are FUCKING kidding me? What an idiot you are – what an idiot I am! I should have known. You fucking white girls are all the same. You'll do it with anyone then you trap the poor bastard. Well, not me Scarlett, not me. I'm not picking up the tab for the rest of your life, you won't be living in the lap of luxury on my money. Is it even mine? The way you spread your legs for me, I doubt it. I'll tell you this though – just for the avoidance of any doubt. You're having an abortion, you stupid slag. How could this happen? How could this fucking happen?'

It happened because he raped me each and every time he saw me but never used a condom, but all I could do was keep apologising. 'I'm so sorry Ed, I'm so sorry. I haven't slept with any other boys, I promise you, Ed. I'd never do that, I'd never cheat on you. You know I love you.'

'Love me? Christ above. I'll have to sort it out,' he said, sighing. I couldn't stop crying. I wanted the baby now and I would just have to find a way to keep it as well as making sure Mum didn't get what she was desperate for.

Being pregnant wasn't enough for Ed not to have sex with me that day, but he barely said a word. He was rougher than usual, not that it was ever a kind act, and I wondered if he was trying to damage me. It was ironic given that I would have wanted that not so long ago, but now I wanted gentleness, now I wanted to provide a safe haven for my baby. As usual, Ed dropped me off at school and drove away silently, revving his car as if in anger, and leaving me in tears.

When I got home, the atmosphere was so strange. Mum was happy and that was an unusual experience for any of us. 'There she is, there's my little . . . ' she couldn't really find a word. I guess she couldn't say 'little mother' as that would give me a role, so she settled on 'Scarlett.' All that night – not a bingo night, remarkably – she kept smiling over at me while we watched telly. In contrast, Dad had gone to the pub, never saying a word to me.

'You alright Scarlett?' she kept asking. 'Want anything? Cup of tea?' I almost fainted, I don't think she'd ever made me a cup of tea in her life!

'No, I'm alright thanks Mum,' I told her. 'Thanks though.'

'Anything. Anything. You just ask. You know Scarlett, I always thought you'd come good. I know there was all the stuff with the drugs and . . . the other things, but when I looked at you in that hospital and I decided to call my little girl after Scarlett O'Hara, I just knew.'

'Right.' She'd never uttered a word like this to me ever before, but she was in some la-la land where my belly held her future and she could rewrite the past.

Mum's euphoria went on into the next day when we went to the GP and found out that I was five months pregnant. A maternity care plan was put in place, and the doctor didn't look surprised or wary at all when Mum said she would be adopting my baby. I knew I would never allow that but it was best to keep quiet at this stage. She still terrified me, and there was a little voice in my mind saying that if I didn't play along with what she wanted, she'd make sure I didn't get my baby either. She was so nasty as a rule that I wouldn't have been surprised if she had kicked it out of me.

The next day, Ed was waiting in his car after school but I wasn't allowed in, he only spoke to me through the window. I smiled but it hit a stony face.

'You're getting an abortion,' he told me as a cold wave ran through my body. 'Alright? I've sorted it and you better fucking go through with it. Probably cost me a fucking fortune but it'll be worth it to get that little bastard out of you. We'll go to Birmingham – Sunday. I'll meet you here at 9 o'clock. Don't you dare fucking not turn up.' He was so emotionless and angry, with a threatening tone I'd never heard from him before. Off he drove – not even a trip to the Wrekin that day.

I didn't want an abortion, but I had no idea how I would get out of this. I would meet him on Sunday, I was terrified of the consequences if I didn't, and I just hoped a plan would come to me at that point.

Mum needed to tell school I was pregnant so she made an appointment with the headmistress for the following day. I'm not sure she had ever been to my school before, she wasn't exactly the sort to get involved or to attend parents' meetings.

Mrs Wallace sat there, staring at me in disgust, but never addressed a single word to my face. It was all directed at Mum, who was acting totally out of character by being very compliant and accepting.

'I know it's terrible and we're ever so disappointed in our Scarlett,' she smirked, 'but I can assure you words have been exchanged and we just need to move on. We're a very traditional family, Mrs Wallace, so there's no way we could do anything to stop this little soul coming into the world, but you needn't worry – I'll love the bones of this baby.'

'I can't have her in my school,' Mrs Wallace sneered, looking as if she couldn't have cared less about the welfare of any child, least of all mine. 'I can't have other girls thinking that such behaviour, such a consequence to morally bankrupt behaviour, is acceptable in any way. It would completely ruin the reputation I have built here. I don't want other girls behaving the way she has behaved – do you understand?'

'Oh absolutely,' simpered Mum. 'I completely agree. Our Scarlett hasn't been brought up this way so I have *no* idea how she has got herself into such a . . . condition. It's really not on. I just want you to know that I will be stepping in. I'll be adopting this baby and making sure it's brought up well.'

'Just get her out,' sighed Mrs Wallace. 'Just get her out of my school.'

I was sure that there must have been other pupils who had got pregnant while at school over the years – I'd heard lots of rumours of the ones who disappeared over summer holidays and we never saw again – but the head was acting as if it had never happened before. Again, I was the slag, and, again, I would have to pay. I'd never liked high school but I had gone through it on my terms. Now, yet again, I was left with no choice but to do what the adults decided was best for me. Mum left with a grin on her face. She'd told someone else about her plan and she hadn't been challenged. Just like with the GP, it was all accepted or ignored. It was all falling nicely into place for her. I was nothing more than a surrogate and she was only going to have to wait another few months before getting a newborn in her arms.

Dad was keeping away from home a lot so Mum's focus was my baby, she wasn't even that bothered about the stepchildren. Apart from the 'adoption', her only other plan was to send me to a different school.

'It's for bad kids,' she told me, smiling. 'You'll fit right in. You've only to go for a couple of hours a day so you'll have plenty of other time to waste. Just keep that baby safe.'

I was to start the following week, but, in the meantime, I had to get through Sunday. I waited outside the closed school gates and Ed picked me up at the agreed time. I just wanted to scream *I'm keeping my baby* but I knew better. No plan had come to me, but I was still desperately hoping that the abortion wouldn't happen. He was so nice to me on the way and I foolishly thought that he might be coming around to the idea of us becoming a little family together.

'Ed,' I began, 'are you sure this is the right thing to do?'

'The abortion?' he asked. I nodded. 'Are you fucking serious? It's the ONLY thing to do, Scarlett! My family would go fucking crazy me if they knew I had even been with you – but you getting yourself pregnant? They would fucking kill me.' I went along with it, I didn't want to upset him. I would just take every moment as it came, hoping against hope that it would all be fine.

We got to the clinic after a drive of about an hour. I'd been allowed to sit in the front as most of the trip was on the motorway and I never mentioned the possibility of having the baby again. We walked into the reception room and I signed in, before a nurse came out, smiling.

'Hello Scarlett,' she said in a really friendly manner. I took to her right away – she was quite short and round, and I just wanted her to scoop me up and say she'd deal with everything in just the way I wanted. 'You OK, love?' I nodded nervously. Ed was watching me the whole time and I think she must have noticed that there was quite an age gap between us. 'You the father?' she asked him.

'Why d'you need to know?' he replied.

'Just asking. Come on Scarlett,' she said, putting her arm around me gently, 'come through with me and we'll see what's what.'

Ed started to follow me, but she took her arm off me and put it in front of him. 'No, just ladies, thanks.'

'I'd rather be there,' he told her.

'Well, that might be the case but you're staying here. I don't even know if you're the dad after all − remember? Cheerio.'

I could have kissed her. I didn't want him there. I didn't even know what was going to happen − was she going to give me an abortion there and then? − but I didn't want Ed to be any part of it.

As soon as we got into the little room, she asked me, 'what do you want to do, love?'

I crumpled immediately. 'I want to keep the baby.'

'OK, OK,' she assured me. 'That's fine − you don't have to do anything you don't want. Is that the father out there, the one who didn't want to answer me? Mr Enigma?' I nodded. 'And is he alright with your decision one way or the other?' I couldn't answer that.

She squeezed my hand. 'Why don't you just sit here a little longer, Scarlett? I've got some paperwork to do in the back office. You gather your thoughts, then we can go back out to reception.'

That's exactly what we did.

'Fixed?' Ed said, throwing down the magazine he'd been reading.

I looked at the nurse.

'Scarlett is fine,' she said. 'You look after her – whoever you are.' She gave me a warm smile when I left and said, 'good luck.' As soon as we got to the car, Ed asked, 'is that it sorted then?' I nodded. I think he assumed that I'd been given a date to go back. In my mind it was sorted – I had left the clinic with my baby still there, and that was what I had wanted out of the appointment. I was allowed to sit in the front seat again with the understanding that I would have to get out before we got to Telford and hide in the back as usual, but, once we were halfway home, I messed up. I told him.

'Ed – I'm keeping the baby.'

'You're what?'

'You heard me. The nurse in there was really nice and she said it's my choice, she said everything would be fine. I want the baby. I want my baby. I'm not going back for an abortion so please don't ask me.' I didn't even have a chance to take another breath before he punched me in the side of the head. The other side of my head hit the passenger window and I saw stars.

'You stupid fucking bitch,' Ed hissed. 'Don't think this is the end of it. You're having a fucking abortion whether you like it or not. That kid will never see the light of day.'

I tried to keep my tears silent, not wanting to anger him further, but the pain was excruciating. He had just been surprised by my decision, I told myself. He wasn't violent, he'd never lifted a finger to me before, so it was totally out of character. We'd get through this, he'd come around to the idea. After all, even I hadn't wanted this baby to start with and now look at me. He dropped me off at the school gates as always, and I bent down at his side of the car. 'It'll be fine, Ed, it'll be fine.'

He stared back at me as if I was a complete stranger. 'Listen to me, Scarlett. This isn't going to happen, but until you make the right fucking decision and get rid of it, tell no one. I'll be letting everyone know what a dirty slag you are. You won't be able to move without every guy I know telling you exactly the sort of filthy bitch you are. And they'll tell their mates who will tell their mates. They'll tell their brothers and their dads and their grandfathers and their uncles. You will be nothing – but you can still make the right choice, it's just that you've really pissed me off today. If this does get out, good luck convincing anyone that I've anything to do with your little bastard. I'll tell all of Telford that you'd screwed every guy here. Don't forget – you belong to me and you'll do everything I say. You fucked up this time Scarlett, but I might give you another chance, we'll see.' With that, he sped off.

From the Monday after that, I knew he had been true to his word. When I went to school, or left to go home, there would be Pakistani boys everywhere. It was as if he had them positioned.

'Look, it's the slag, it's the prostitute, it's the whore,' they would shout, even little boys who looked like they should be in primary school. I felt it was more targeted than ever. Previously, it was more of a 'white girls are trash' type of insult, but I really did feel now that they had been told to say these things to me. I know that some people want to make out it's racist if you say anything about what is said to girls in those areas, then and now, but I can say with hand on heart that most of the insults had 'white' in front of them. We were always treated as if we were rubbish, as if we were there to be humiliated just because we were white. I never saw one of the girls from those families called the things that were thrown at us. I don't think it's racist to say that – I think it's racist to deny it. If every insult had been prefaced with something about a mental or physical disability, would it not be seen as bigoted, as there for a reason, as there to demean? Of course it would, and it should. So why would this be any different? We were slags because we were white and we were trash because of the colour of our skin – because of that, we were disposable and we had to take it.

If I was with a friend, they'd call, 'Stay away from the slut!' It was such a tight-knit community and it soon spread that I was the white whore you could say anything to. Even lads on their own would verbally abuse me, old men in traditional dress – there were no barriers. They would ask for blow jobs, hand jobs, tell me to bend over, say they would fuck me any way I could imagine, and that I would live it all because I was nothing, I was just trash on the street. All I wanted was for Ed to rush in and protect me, tell them we were a couple – how deluded is that?

It wasn't long before everyone could tell that I was pregnant anyway. I had few friends but I had met a woman called Ellen who was a friend of my sister, Jackie (who had moved out by now). She was about ten years older than me and her house became a safe haven. It got me away from Mum constantly going on about the adoption as well as giving me somewhere to hide when all of the name calling got too much. Unfortunately, it was on Regent Street. Ellen was one of the few white people living there but she kept herself to herself and didn't cause or receive much trouble. Sure, she was a white slag too in their eyes, but it didn't have the hatred behind it that they saved for me. I would run the gauntlet of young and old men calling me horrible names to get to her house and just collapse on the sofa.

'Fuckers,' I would say, pretending to be brave when my heart was pounding. I really thought they would all set on me one day as their loathing seemed almost tangible.

'Ignore them, babe,' Ellen would say. 'They're like that to all of us. They wouldn't know how else to be as we're just shit to them.'

One day, when I was about seven months pregnant, I had gone to Ellen's house after my usual two hours at school. I'd been there for ages and it was getting dark, so I had to get going. I'd walked halfway down the street when I heard someone run up behind me. I felt a punch to the back of my head then, before I could process what was happening, someone had me on the ground and was beating the shit out of me. I was kicked and punched in my face, my back – and my stomach. Mostly my stomach. They were relentless. I tried to protect my belly and was terrified that this man, whoever he was, had hurt my baby. I was shouting out to him that I had nothing to steal, I didn't even have a purse with me, but it made no difference. Finally, as blood streamed down my face, the man in black ran off.

I was in shock and, to this day, have no idea how I got home. I went straight to bed – there was no one in who I could tell – and fell asleep in fear and exhaustion.

When I woke the next morning, my eyes were swollen to the point where they wouldn't even open. I couldn't see a thing. Mum came in and started screaming.

'Oh God! What's happened to you, Scarlett? What have you done?'

'I haven't done anything!' I told her. 'I was beaten up.'

'My baby, my baby!' she screamed. 'Is my baby OK?'

'Not really – I can't even open my eyes,' I told her, surprised at her concern.

'Not you,' she snapped. 'I couldn't give a flying fuck about you. I mean *my* baby – have you been bleeding? Are you cramping?'

It was what I was worried about too, but I wasn't sure. No, there wasn't blood or cramping, but I'd been beaten shitless, so how could the baby possibly be alright? Mum called the police and the GP surgery, who sent a midwife out. She got there first and checked the baby's heartbeat and movements, reassuring me that everything was fine. The police took a statement and photos of my face but I couldn't tell them everything, I couldn't tell them how Regent Street had been for me for almost a year now.

They worked out quite quickly who was behind it and I was surprised to discover it was actually a girl, a friend of Ellen's. She was taken to court and found guilty, her defence being that I had been having an affair with her husband. I didn't even know who she was. In later years, she told me that Ed had paid her to do it, to try and make me miscarry, but I guess I'd always suspected that as I'd been hit in my stomach so much, it had seemed so targeted.

I never went anywhere apart from school and, occasionally, the local youth club. I felt quite safe there as I always tagged along with my sister, Jackie. I tried to join in, but I was always on edge, never knowing when Ed would catch me on the street, or if he would send someone after me.

One night, when I was about eight months pregnant, I was sitting in a corner with Jackie and I couldn't help but cry. I felt so alone and Mum was really piling on the pressure about adopting my baby. I swore to myself that it would never happen, but she was acting like it was a foregone conclusion. I had no idea what would happen and the birth was looming.

'You'll be OK – you're always OK,' said Jackie with little sympathy. 'Your problem is that you've always been so protected from everything, Dad's golden girl. You're having to face the real world now.' I couldn't even begin to process how wrong she was and I wondered had she completely forgotten what I had asked her that day when I wanted to know if he was doing to her what he did to me?

Her friend Jed was there too. He was 18, from Cyprus originally, and a really nice lad who was always happy to play board games or listen to music with us when we were at the club.

'Come on Jackie,' he said, 'a little kindness towards your baby sister wouldn't go amiss.' He rubbed my back. 'She just doesn't know how to show she cares.' I doubted that she cared at all, but it was nice of him to try and make out that she did. 'You need a change, let's get a bit of fresh air, it'll clear your head.'

We went outside and I told him all of my worries. Well, I told him *some* of them. No one knew about Ed, no one knew the real circumstances of how my baby had been conceived.

'It must be hard,' said Jed. 'Where I come from, family stick together. I do think that Jackie wants to help but doesn't feel she can. I think she'll come around. Do you want to go for a walk? Get some chips?'

I confided a bit more in him as we walked. As we passed by the local park, there was a little shed there where the workmen often sat and drank their tea. It was always open, there was nothing to steal, and, before I knew it – in the middle of me talking – Jed pushed me in.

'What are you doing?' I gasped.

'Don't worry, I'll be quick,' he laughed, grabbing at my dress, pushing it up my legs.

'Jed! No! What are you even thinking of!'

'I'm pretty sure you know, Scarlett, or you wouldn't be in the condition you're in, would you?' He pushed my knickers to the side and all I could think was, *my baby, you're going to hurt my baby.* He didn't care. He just did what they all did. Everywhere I went, there were men waiting to do that to me.

'You coming back to youth club?' he asked me when he was done. I shook my head. 'OK – thanks, Scarlett. See you around.' And off he went. That was it again. As had been the case so many times before, since I was only eight, I was left with the shame that should have been theirs. His filth was running down my legs but he'd had a nice time, so that was all that mattered, right? When would I learn that they were all the same, when would I learn?

I know you're scared, Scarlett, and you have been from the second you suspected you had this little human growing inside of you. I know you don't want anything to happen to this baby, I know that you would give him the world if you could. I know that you have protected him through rape and beatings already but you still have some protecting to do. I know you still don't trust anyone so you still don't talk, I want you to know that I believe in you, I have always believed in you and you will get through this, you are strong and you are a fighter. Before you know it, you'll have someone else to fight for too. You need to keep your baby from your mother and you need to keep your baby by your side as much as you can. This won't be easy and I won't lie

– you won't always manage it. But keep your eye on what needs to happen here in this moment. Stay on your own, have your baby, then prepare for the combat ahead.

Chapter Eight

Danny

By the time I was approaching full-term, Mum could barely contain her excitement. While I lay on the sofa, exhausted and huge, she would be dancing around, singing, telling me that she couldn't wait to be there when 'her' baby was born. She bought the pram she wanted, the cot she wanted and the baby clothes she wanted. It really didn't seem to penetrate her brain that I was the one having this baby.

'My baby, my baby, I just can't wait for my baby!' she would croon, touching my tummy and making kissing noises to it. She'd never willingly been affectionate with me in my life before, but I had something she wanted now. The problem was, I wanted it too.

I knew she was taking Philip and Mark, the foster kids, to London to see their parents one Friday evening and I just hoped that, by some stroke of luck, that would be the weekend my baby would come. I couldn't quite believe it when, on the Friday afternoon, I started having contractions. By 8pm, they were only five minutes apart but I needed to hold on until 9pm as that was when she was leaving. It was agony and she seemed to be hanging around me, so I just gritted my teeth and did some deep breathing whenever she left the room. I swear I kept that baby in by sheer willpower!

I could finally move into the pain once she left. She didn't seem as happy to be with the foster kids as she usually was and she keep warning me not to go into labour while she was gone – little did she know that, within an hour of her departure, I'd called an ambulance. As soon as I got to hospital, I could be honest about the pain to someone else.

'The baby's coming!' I told the first midwife I saw. 'My baby is almost here.'

She examined me and said wearily, 'I'm not too sure about that love, let's check again in a few hours.'

A few hours! I was convinced this baby was going to appear any second! At midnight, they looked again. I was only 2cm dilated. I thought that maybe I was so keen to get the little one out without Mum being there that I had convinced myself it would happen in a flash. The only thing I wondered about was that I had a high pain threshold – it had been well-cultivated over the years – so I couldn't quite work out why I had been in such unbearable pain since that afternoon.

'Babies come when they're ready,' said a midwife. She meant well, but I needed this baby now. 'You really need to rest,' she added. 'I think you've got a long labour ahead of you so it would be better if you could prepare for that.' I couldn't rest! I had to get my baby out! 'You'll be too exhausted by the time you need to push. Trust me,' she said. 'You need something to help you sleep.

Just after midnight, I relented – and slept solidly for 8 hours. When I woke up, the pain was intense and I laboured for four hours before it happened. The most wonderful moment in my life so far.

My baby.

My little boy.

Danny was born at 12.20pm on the Saturday. I felt I had wasted some of those hours of Mum being away, but as I looked at his perfect face, I couldn't think of anything else but how incredible he was. I just wanted to be left alone with him and the midwives and had no idea until much later that my brother had found out I was in labour and had sat outside the delivery room for hours, even while I was asleep before it all kicked off properly.

I had done it. I was so proud and he was the most beautiful thing I had ever seen but, already, there was a lurking fear about what waited for me outside. I needed to leave that house, to get away from everyone who had hurt me, to be happy and find peace. Perfection didn't exist, I knew that, but I would have to ignore the names they called me as I tried to make a life for me and my baby. They would hurt but I would have him as a shield.

I had been ripped apart by the birth but I didn't care. I adored Danny from that very first second. He was like something out of a baby book and I couldn't believe that I had made him. He had olive skin and thick dark hair – obviously Ed's baby and that brought me such fear. What if he came for him? I had been worried about Mum, worried about Dad, but it had never crossed my mind until now that Ed might decide to take our child.

Mum turned up sooner than I expected – I guess there were plenty of people who could have told her. She was carrying three teddies and the clothes she had bought for Danny.

'Trust you,' she said, 'you never do anything right.' I guess I wasn't the wonderful Scarlett who did amazing things any longer. 'I told you not to go into labour when I wasn't there. Oh my God though, look at him!' I think, apart from sleeping, I had kept Danny in my arms from the moment I'd had him, but she'd put an end to that. 'Give him here,' she said, snatching him from me. 'Look at you, look at my little baby!' she kept saying.

'He's not yours, Mum, he's mine.'

'Don't be ridiculous – how would you look after a baby?'

'I would learn. I'd read all the books and I'd get help from school, they help lots of girls like me who have babies when they're young.'

'Do they help the stupid ones?' she mocked. 'You know, you've been lucky here, Scarlett, but don't fuck things up now.'

'What do you mean, I've been lucky?'

'Well, he looks Greek really. All that dark hair and tanned skin.'

'As opposed to what?' I asked her.

'Don't act daft with me. I've heard the rumours – I've been told to my face actually. You've been hanging around Regent Street for months. And we all know what type lives there.'

'What type, Mum? What type? And be careful now, because that's your grandson you're partly talking about,' I warned her.

Her anger started to come to the surface – it was so hard for her to keep up this particular act. 'You don't get to tell me to be careful, madam. You've been shagging half of Regent Street so I doubt you even know who the dad is. Now, what are we going to call you, my perfect baby boy?' she cooed.

'Danny. He's called Danny,' I told her firmly.

'Is he fuck. I never agreed to that.'

'Funnily enough, you don't get a say,' I snapped, 'because I'm his mummy, not you. And you won't even be his granny unless you behave yourself.'

I saw her hand fly up to hit me, just as a midwife came in.

'Alright, Scarlett?' she asked, looking at Mum who quickly plastered a smile on her face. 'Alright Granny? This your first then?'

'That I know of, ha ha!' she laughed, back to performing. 'Gorgeous, isn't he? I can't wait to get him home – think I'll be stealing him and pretending he's mine!'

'Well, the great thing about being a granny is that you can get all the hugs but none of the bad stuff. You'll be glad to hand him back and avoid all of that!'

'Oh, I don't think so,' said Mum. 'Scarlett and I have agreed that this one will just be like another one of mine! Just need to get him a nice name and then take him home.'

'I thought he was called Danny?' said the midwife. 'That's a lovely name.'

'No,' Mum resisted. 'Nothing's been decided yet.'

I finally found my tongue. 'Yes, you're right. It's Danny.'

Mum looked daggers at me as the midwife said, 'It suits him. Just got to do a few boring tests on you, Scarlett, and check Danny's OK, then you can get a rest. Hand him back then, Granny. And she won't be coming home that soon – she'll be in for 10 days as she's had a hard time and needs to heal. Plenty of time to bond though, which is always lovely.'

Mum was not happy. If she'd been allowed to stay alone with me for longer, she would have tried to wear me down, but she wasn't in charge here, the midwives were. I was so glad Mum had left but knew I would have to face her at some point. Not all of the midwives were as nice as the one who had subtly put Mum in her place. When one came in later, she saw the teddies at the bottom of my bed and asked me who they were for?

'What do you mean?' I asked.

'You or the baby?' she laughed. 'You probably still play with those at your age, don't you?' I honestly felt that was her way of calling me a slag. I was young, I was unmarried, I'd just had a baby – she had made up her mind about me, just as I was sure many others would. In fact, when I was discharged from the ward, the Matron said to me, 'I was actually dreading having you here – 15 and a baby. But do you know what, Scarlett? You could put some of these older mothers to shame. Keep it up, Danny will be fine. You'll be great at this, I know you will.'

That meant a lot to me. I had spent the time with Danny since his birth doing everything I could for him and taking all the advice I was given, but I was dreading going back home. Mum had, of course, visited – as had Dad, who said very little – and had kept at me with her constant framing of herself as the one who would be looking after and bringing up my child. There were days when I felt more able to argue with her than others, but my heart stayed strong and when she left, I would always hold my baby close and tell him that I was his mummy, and that I would never let her adopt him. Ed had never been near me or his son, and I wasn't surprised as he wouldn't want to run the chance of being there with anyone else, but I still had that underlying fear that he would try and take Danny from me at some point.

When I got home with him, it was as if Mum had been nursing all of her frustration and annoyance for 10 days. I was barely in the door when she grabbed Danny off me, changing her tone as soon as she got him. Her voice was dripping with hatred for me, but she was all sweetness and light with him. I wouldn't have minded that if she hadn't been so clear during the pregnancy that she wanted to adopt him.

'You listen to me,' she snarled. 'If you want to pick my baby up, you ask me. If he needs feeding, I'll do it. If he needs changing, I'll do it. If you want to do anything at all with him, I'll be the one who decides whether it will happen, not you. Understand?'

'I need permission to pick up my own baby?' I asked her incredulously.

'No, you need permission to pick up *my* baby,' she smiled. 'You're a kid. And you're a slag. The best chance this little darling has is me.'

I tried. I really did try, but if he was crying and I went to him, she'd scream at me whether she was in the room or sensed it from somewhere else.

'Leave him alone! You've got no right to do that!' she'd yell. 'He hates you anyway, surely you can see that?' I was starting to wonder. She was there for him so often and so quickly that I thought he probably was confused, and the longer she managed to keep it going, perhaps she would finally manage to make him think she was his mum. She was barely ever at bingo, and she had sent Mark and Philip back to London, so she really did seem to be deluded about this fantasy of hers becoming reality. She took over, constantly telling me that I was a kid, I was a slut, that I probably didn't even know who the father was, but, actually, it was only about six weeks after Danny was born that I would turn sixteen.

She never mentioned Mark and Philip, they had been forgotten as soon as she had a new child in her sights, but one day there was a knock on our door and, before I knew it, there were five people in our living room. It turned out that they were all social workers and police officers – and they were there because of Mark, the little boy who had touched himself.

He had been at nursery back home in London when he began drawing pictures which worried the staff enormously. These pictures were of someone he called Brian and they were horrific illustrations of things he was saying, in his words, of what the bad man had done. The social services knew that Mark had stayed with us – and that Dad was called Brian. One police officer stood beside me the whole time the others were asking questions of Mum. Dad was working abroad at the time, so he wasn't even part of it.

'Is that your baby?' she whispered, looking over at Danny in a Moses basket near Mum.

'Yes, yes he's mine,' I told her.

'Gorgeous. Do me a favour, love. Quick as you can, nip over and grab him, then get in the police car outside. I'll be right behind you.' She didn't need to ask me twice, I flew over to Danny, picked him up and the bottle that was lying on the side of the sofa by the Moses basket, and run out of the room.

'Where the fuck is she going with that baby?' screamed Mum, but the policewoman was right behind me and she bundled me into a car while another one held Mum back to prevent her from following me. I could hear her ranting and raving inside, but I was driven to the local police station before anything else happened. Immediately, I was taken to one of the little side rooms where they conduct interviews, and a social worker came in after a few minutes. I had no idea what was going on and kept cradling Danny, so relieved that I had him with me.

'You can't go back home, Scarlett,' the social worker told me. 'I'm sorry, but that just won't be something we can let happen at the moment.'

'Sorry?' I said. 'I'm not really bothered, but all of Danny's stuff is there – can you get things for me?' She nodded. 'And where will we go? Where will I go with my baby?'

'Well, because of your age, you'll have to go into foster care for a bit. You'll be together with Danny though.'

My head was spinning. Dad had always told me that police would take me away and I'd end up somewhere else, and now that was happening, but I didn't understand why. It wasn't long before I found out. A policeman was next through the door, and before he'd even sat down, he said, 'We know that's your dad's baby,' pointing at Danny. 'Tell us the truth.'

I wasn't speaking to anyone from that point, not about details. It was clear that Mark had made allegations of abuse, but why were they jumping to thinking Dad had fathered Danny? Did they know he had been at me for years? I refused to speak to either the police or the social workers. They could see my baby's heritage, they could see his father must be Pakistani, which my own dad clearly was not.

I only asked for one thing. My friend Louise's mum was a foster carer and I wanted to go to her. They agreed and I went there that very night. Vivienne was fantastic. She showed me how to make up bottles for Danny, which I had never been allowed to do. She seemed surprised that I was clueless about that but I just muttered something about Mum always helping me − not the truth about never being allowed and never actually having fed my own baby since hospital − and she kindly gave me all the lessons I needed.

While I was staying with Vivienne and Louise, the social worker who now had me and Danny as one of her cases started giving me £15 a week. To me, that was a fortune. I'd never really had any money of my own before and the first thing I wanted to do was go out and enjoy myself. Louise and I would go into town and get drunk on cheap cider as often as we could, and it didn't take long for my life to spiral out of control. My life was back to where it had left off really. Vivienne was nicer than Mum, of course, and she would never hurt Danny, so I had no worries leaving him with her to go into town. When I got back, paralytic, she would have all the night-time feeds made up for me and I stumbled about in the night, still drunk, but always alert to Danny needing fed.

It might be hard for people to understand why I had gone to that sort of life, why I had started staying out and drinking when I had a baby at the house of a foster carer. All I can say is, my whole life had been ripped apart in minutes when the police turned up. As much as I hated that house and everyone in it, that's all I had ever known, so taking me away really screwed with my head. I was put into a normal functional family; they had meals at the table together, they asked how everyone had been, what their day had been like, and it was all completely alien to me. I actually needed to escape, but the one thing there was that I knew Danny was safe. I could go out and get pissed whilst knowing that they didn't want to take him away from me. Vivienne was looking after him properly, if that makes sense, and that allowed me to find an escape in alcohol.

Louise and I would usually get drunk in the toilets at the bus station as they were always empty. Once we were pissed enough, we'd go down the steps at the side and that little lane would take you to the local churchyard. I had gone right back to being recognised when I was out, and even on the walk from the bus station toilets to the churchyard, there would be men shouting 'slag' at me. Louise and I would sit there, drinking more, and making plans for our future that would never happen. I was only 16, but I knew enough of life already to realise that I was making castles in the sky. We'd stagger from the churchyard back through the streets to Louise's house, holding onto each other and often giving as good as we got to the men who were calling us all the white trash names that came from their mouths constantly.

It was on one of these nights that Ed drove past. I hadn't seen him since Danny was born and would go between the fear that he would try to take my baby one day, and another level of fear that I would never see him again.

'Oi! Scarlett!' he shouted, as if he'd only seen me the day before. 'Get in then – you and your mate. Get in and I'll give you a lift.' I automatically went to the back seat and hissed at Louise to do the same. Old habits die hard after all. 'Crouch down,' I said, and we sat in the footwells so no one who knew Ed could see us. He took us back to Louise's house but when we got there, told her to get out while he spoke to me. She staggered in, not needing to be told twice, desperate to collapse into her bed.

'You stay here though, Scarlett – you stay here.' He wanted me, I knew that. He would have sent me in too if it was truly just a lift. In desperation and hope, I blurted everything out and he was so caring. 'You've really been through it, haven't you?' he said. Then he did something he had never done before – he clambered over to the back seat and just held me. Held me in his arms and stroked my hair. It was all I wanted, all I had wanted for so long.

'Scarlett,' he whispered. 'I'm really sorry you've been through all of this – but can you suck my dick?'

And did I? Of course I did – I was right back to where I had been with that too. And when Ed said to leave it with him, that he would see what he could do about a house, my romantic mind convinced me that he meant us moving in somewhere as a family. I still had hope. I wonder now how that could possibly be. Why did I think that someone whose only idea of a relationship was to get me to give him a blow job after giving birth to his son, was the love of my life?

I never really told anyone about Dad, I never thought I could trust anyone. When you are told you will be blamed and then someone actually does come into the house and takes you away, you believe it's your fault, even when you have a baby of your own and you're 16 years old. I wondered how they couldn't see that. They were having meetings about me and finally decided I could go back home as long as Dad wasn't there. I didn't know what I wanted, but I was aware that Louise's mum only took short-term placements so I would be out on my ear soon anyway. So, I went back – they kept to their word and Dad was nowhere to be seen. I assumed that he had been sent to some sort of temporary accommodation until Mum told me the truth.

'They questioned the dirty old bastard,' she said, 'but do you know what that arsehole did? Turns out he hadn't been abroad when they came here after all. He'd been with his tart in Blackpool all along! He's been shagging some other woman for God knows how long – and here's me with fucking police and social workers at my door.' She couldn't have thought he was an angel but Mum did seem shocked by what had transpired. 'So, I'm sitting here thinking I'll give him hell when he gets back, and guess what?' I had no idea. 'He never fucking came back! He's pissed off to live with her!'

It was fantastic news for me – one parent down, one to go – but it meant that there was still no closure. Still, I had Danny and my baby was all I needed.

There is a lot I want to tell you here, Scarlett, because you're heading for a bad place, a very bad place. It's OK to be scared now that you have this little one to protect. You are worrying

*for two. **Asking for help isn't a sign of weakness,
there are people that care and would probably go
out of their way to protect you both, but you've
been let down so many times you just don't know
who to trust anymore, do you? Drinking won't
help, it never does. It makes you forget things in
that moment but the next day, when you wake
up, everything that is wrong in your life is still
wrong. You're not listening though, are you?
You're closing off, shutting down. Just focus on
that baby – if you can do that, then maybe you're
not heading for the place I fear.***

Chapter Nine

Always there

I'd been home for about a month and my meet-ups with Ed were regular occurrences. They were always in his car and we always had sex, whether it was him on top grunting away, or me giving him a blow job that he barely even acknowledged. He'd only ever seen Danny in an offhand way if he stopped the car when I was out walking with the pram and showed very little interest. The first time this happened, he was completely unengaged. There was a muttered 'boy or girl?' as he peered in the pram. When I confirmed the former, he said, 'nice,' then went on his way. It was hardly the moment I had waited for, but I explained it to myself as him not being able to say much in case someone saw us.

I convinced myself that he was working hard to find somewhere for us all to live and it finally seemed as if I'd been right.

'Got you somewhere,' he announced one night after rolling off me. 'Got a place for you and the baby.' He was clearly pleased with himself and so was I. He'd done this for us and I knew that what he really wanted was to step up and to provide for us all. I genuinely couldn't see any other motive. 'Meet me tomorrow and I'll take you to have a look round.'

I couldn't wait! This would make up for the hard times, when I was alone and when I thought no one would ever love me. I'd stop drinking and I'd put some distance between me and Mum so that Danny was never around our toxic relationship. I could barely sleep that night and every time I got my baby boy on my own, I would tell him how good his daddy was and what a lovely life we'd have together.

The next day, I met Ed as planned. The house was in an area that must have been 90% Pakistani but that was fine – after all, my boyfriend had just as much right to make sure his child was around his culture too. I swore that I would never let Danny become one of those boys who stood on street corners shouting obscenities at white girls though. Even though he was half-Pakistani, he also had me and that would stop him following those boys and copying them. He would respect me and he would be brought up in a family where men and women were equals.

'It's perfect,' I told Ed as we walked around. It wasn't. It was very, very basic – furnished, but with nothing nice. Everything was on its last legs, with peeling formica and stained walls. There was a bed and settee, a cooker splattered in grease, and it all needed a good scrub, but it was ours. 'I'll make it lovely. We'll be happy here,' I told him. 'Just the three of us.'

'Three of us?' he laughed. 'What? You bringing a mate to stay? You can't think I'm moving in, Scarlett. Here? With you? With the kid? Christ, I couldn't have people thinking that. I'll only be 10 doors down though. I'll come and see you all the time.'

Holding the tears back, I just nodded. I'd always known that his parents were very traditional – to the extent that I had only ever seen his mum out of the house on two or three occasions – and if I needed to just accept that Ed couldn't be with me quite yet, I would. Maybe I could eventually go to his house, meet his mother and introduce her to Danny? She'd surely love to know about her grandson under the right circumstances, then when she got to know me too, it would be easier for Ed to leave his family home and we'd all be together.

'OK,' I told him, 'OK.' I also made a mental commitment to try and understand his culture more. I wanted him to so I would try to be like them. Those men and boys who shouted at me, they were probably just grandstanding. I'm sure the others would like me once I was seen as Ed's girlfriend and the mother of his child. It was a completely foolish thing to even think, but I was blinded by love and I just wanted Ed with me all the time to chase the perfect life I dreamed could really be mine if I worked out the best way to act and behave.

Predictably, Mum was incandescent with rage when I told her we were moving out. 'You're taking my baby?' she yelled. 'I don't fucking think so.' But she had to fucking think so when I picked up the few things I had and left. 'You won't get away with this!' she warned me, 'you needn't think I'm going to let you do this, Scarlett!'

I walked away with a smile on my face. I had my baby and I would soon have my man, but within a week she'd found a way to challenge everything. Mum had a close friend who was a health visitor and this woman turned up on my doorstep one day. With no acknowledgement that she knew me, she simply said, 'I'm here to check Baby Jones. We've had reports he's being neglected. I'd be obliged if you'd let me see him, please.'

'Debbie,' I said, 'You know Danny, you've seen him at Mum's. What is this all about?'

'As I've said, Miss Jones, there have been reports. If you could please let me in to see the baby, that would be the first step.'

'Fill your boots,' I told her. 'He's asleep in his pram, he's been bathed and fed, and he's far from neglected thanks for asking.'

Debbie looked him over, clearly desperately trying to find fault. She sniffed in displeasure, looking round the room. It was tatty, I knew that, but I was trying to do a little bit of cleaning every day and hoping that Ed would give me some money soon to buy a few nice things. 'This isn't a very nice place to bring up a baby, is it?' she said.

'I'm sure you've seen worse. Never mind the décor, did Mum send you here?'

'Your mother is also a concerned grandmother,' she snapped. 'She wanted the world for that baby, as you well know. She is an excellent foster carer,' (there was no mention of Mark I noticed), 'and instead of being involved in his life day and night, she watches you smoking and drinking and sleeping around. You're very lucky to have her.' With that, she flounced off.

She reported me to Social Services almost immediately. At their first visit, I was told Danny would be taken away immediately if I messed up. I was doing my best and I was doing OK, or so I'd thought. Mum's spitefulness had set me back but I'd just have to prove to everyone that I was looking after Danny.

Until he was one and I was 17, things trundled along. Ed was coming to the house now and giving me as little money as he could get away with despite him always having nice clothes and a lovely car for himself. He never stayed for more than about thirty minutes at a time – and that included sex and a bit of playtime with Danny. I pretended to myself that it was fantastic, but it was next to nothing. I hadn't really been able to do anything with the house as it was a shit tip even underneath the grime, and I had fallen back into drinking whenever Louise came to see me, bringing cheap wine or cider. All I did was wait every day in case Ed would deign to come by and give us a scrap of his life. I rarely went out for fear that I would miss his visit and would sit at the window praying that he would walk up the path any minute.

The house was very close to the one that he had taken me to on that very first meeting when I was 14, and I was starting to notice that there were a few that looked very similar when I went on brief walks with Danny, and even a few on my street. The general upkeep of the area was poor – in particular, no one seemed to have nice gardens – but there was an even worse look to these other houses. There would sometimes be a limp net curtain at one of the windows, there would always be high weeds outside or it had been flattened by concrete, and it would be clear that no families lived in them. I'd often see men go in and out, but not for long. At night, I would hear car doors banging pretty much constantly and there seemed to be a steady stream of visitors, I assumed it was a drug den.

Ed's family was very traditional but it was superficial. His mum always walked well behind his dad on the few times I saw her out. She was almost fully covered and never spoke. The father would stop and chat to other men while she waited, submissively. He had lots of brothers – I'm not even sure how many – and would often shout to one of them when he was going in and out of mine, so I assumed they knew who I was. They were also part of the groups who would stand on street corners or shout out of cars at white girls. Given that I knew there was not only this behaviour, but that it must be known locally and even in his family, I wouldn't have been surprised if the houses were indeed being used for drugs.

Ed drank, despite being a Muslim, and I knew from the way he treated me that he was obsessed with sex. It was hardly the behaviour of a devoutly religious family, but they put on a show. I also knew that his sister, Aliyah, was perfectly aware of me and Danny. She would stare at us when we went on a walk, but never spoke to me or my son. The fact that she would stand outside and watch the house or be there when I was going out convinced me that she had been told by Ed – or someone else – about the situation. He confirmed it when I confronted him one day but just said, 'don't worry, she won't say anything, she knows her place.'

I wasn't worried about her telling their parents – in fact, I wanted her to. If it all came out into the open, I was still convinced that I could win them all round. Danny was a lovely baby, a beautiful child, and I was sure they would be proud of him.

I'd been there for a few months, playing pretend happy families, when Ed turned up quite late one night with another man while Danny was in bed, fast asleep for the night. He must have been in his mid-20s, so a bit older than Ed, and I didn't think I had ever seen him before. I would have remembered actually, as he was one of the ugliest creatures I'd come across in a long time.

'This is Asad,' Ed told me. 'His dad owns the house. This is Scarlett,' he told Asad, smiling. I was so pleased – finally, he was introducing me to his friends! Asad wasn't good-looking in the slightest. He had black, greasy hair, and, as he stood close to me, the stench of body odour was overpowering. I tried to subtly put my hand up to my nose and not breathe in.

'Show him round,' said Ed.

'Haven't you been here before?' I asked. 'If your dad owns it?'

'Just show him round, don't fucking interrogate him.'

I wasn't quite sure how to do that. It was small and not exactly a palace, but I tried. 'Well, you're standing in the living room,' I giggled, 'and if you want to go through there, you'll be in the kitchen.'

'Take him upstairs, give him the full tour,' said Ed. Asad wasn't saying a word and didn't look as if he particularly wanted to be showing interest in some grim rooms.

'I don't really want to risk waking Danny,' I answered.

'Tough shit.'

The three of us went up and I just opened the door very slightly to my room. 'Not much to see, really.' There wasn't. The bed was basic, the mattress was a lumpy old thing, and I didn't even have a wardrobe so my clothes were all over the floor. I was a bit embarrassed by it really. Ed was behind me and, in a flash, he had pushed me in.

'Sort him out,' he said, as Asad followed me in.

I knew exactly what he meant. *Sort me out*, was often the phrase he used when he wanted a blow job or sex from me. I looked at him in horror. 'No, Ed – I don't want to!'

'As. If. That. Fucking. Matters. Do it. You're not exactly a virgin, are you?' His eyes looked the way they had when he punched me in the head in the car after the journey to the abortion clinic and I knew that if I didn't do what he was demanding, that would happen again. It was as clear as that and as quick as that. I knew this man had violence bubbling under the surface and I didn't want to risk it, not with Danny fast asleep and vulnerable.

I took a deep breath as Ed closed the door behind me. Asad did nothing more than nod as he pushed me towards the bed. He was just as disgusting and smelly as I feared. He took my clothes off, gripping my breasts so tightly that I thought I would cry out in pain. His fingers were everywhere, just as Dad's used to be, and his roughness was hard to bear. By the time he was ready to penetrate me, I was already in agony. He was heartless, shoving himself into me over and over, as his greasy head pressed against my face. I thought I would retch and it was the thought of Dad that actually reminded me, *you have a place to go, Scarlett, you have your cottage; take yourself there and forget all of this. He'll be done soon, they're always done soon, so just go there, go to where the waves crash and the roses grow.*

I did. I went there while I had sex with this stranger, and, yet again, didn't even process that it was rape. When Asad was finished with me, he gave me a light slap on the side of my face. It wasn't sore, it was more of a jokey one, almost like a fist bump, as if to say, 'thanks mate.' He got off me, and went out to Ed, who must have been sitting outside the bedroom door the whole time. As I lay there, I heard them laughing and joking in Urdu. All of them spoke in Urdu unless it was in direct relation to me. What a great night they'd had.

As I lay there, in the filth that men had always left on me, I realised that it was nothing more than a transaction for them. Ed had loaned me out for a brief time and hadn't even bothered to stay and see if I was OK afterwards. I was numb and all I wanted was to lie in a hot bath for hours. While I soaked in it, I realised I had a new fear. I couldn't really lie here for hours, I had to be quick, just as I used to have to be quick in case Dad came into the bathroom at home. Ed had a key. What if he came back with Asad again? What if he came back with someone else? I felt as if a line had been crossed, so quickly got out, wrapped myself in a towel and ran to the back door which he usually used, locking it and leaving a key in there which I hoped would stop him from entering.

The next day, I went to see Mum. I had been avoiding her as much as I could as I couldn't forgive her for putting me on the radar of social workers, who were still checking up on me regularly. However, I had spent the night thinking about what had happened with Ed and Asad, and now wondered if I should start allowing her in my life more. I had two reasons for this. I knew she would look after Danny well, so if I needed him out of the house, that was the most obvious place to take him. The second reason was, if the social workers found out that I was doing what Ed had forced me into, they might look on me more favourably if I had my mum, the perfect foster parent, in my life. That was a muddled way of thinking, as I didn't know who would be grassing me up, but Danny had to be my first concern.

Ed did bring Asad back a few times and there was no pretence that he was there for any other reason than to fuck me. I don't even know if he could speak English. It was always disgusting. He never smelled any better and I wondered if he even washed at all. There seemed to be a film of dirt on him and I wanted to scrub my skin off with steel wool after he had touched me. Asad was always rough but he was quick. I was nothing more than a hole to him, and he quickly made that clear in the dismissive way he treated me. I hated myself as much as I hated him, but the smile I got from Ed when it was all over convinced me that I was doing it for him. He must be pleased with me, I reckoned, and I must be helping him in some way. There were surely no circumstances under which he would willingly let his girlfriend do that with another man unless he had to. Maybe he was in debt, or maybe I was paying the rent with my body? I'd always find an excuse for him at that time rather than face up to the facts.

Mum had been begging me to let her have Danny for a sleepover and she was actually being quite nice to me with no talk of adoption, so I agreed. I also decided to go out with Louise. I needed to feel like me again so we went to a local pub where I got tipsy but not pissed. I got back at about 10pm and Ed was waiting for me. In the house, on the sofa, with a face like thunder. The moment I walked in, he started screaming.

'Where the hell have you been, you slag? What the fuck have you been doing?

'Nothing, Ed, nothing! I'm so sorry,' I apologised, sobering up in an instant. 'I just had a few drinks with Louise, I thought you wouldn't mind.'

'You been fucking other men? You been in the pub giving blow jobs and hand jobs to all those fucking white losers, you whore?' he shouted. It's hard to describe his face when he was saying this. It had turned so ugly with anger, his teeth were clenched and his fists were in balls at the side of his body.

'I've just been out, I've just been out,' I whispered. 'Please don't be mad.'

'I've sat here for fucking hours. Asad comes round and you're not in? How do you think I explain that? How do you think that makes me look? Like an IDIOT! Like someone who can't control his slag, that's how it makes me look!'

'I'm not a slag, I'm not – please stop saying that.'

'You are fucking joking, right? You fuck my mate without even questioning it, you lie there with him having the time of your miserable fucking life, and you have the nerve to say you're not a slag? Wake up, Scarlett, wake up.'

He launched himself at me, and it was a complete onslaught. Hands turning into fists, kicking and punching as if I was a man rather than a skinny little girl-woman who couldn't fight back. I fell to the floor, curling up in a ball while it all rained down on me, worse than the beating when I was pregnant, worse than anything I could have imagined he would do to me. He hit and hit and hit me. I thought he would never run out of energy and he was clearly enjoying it. His usual insults peppered every blow and I thought he would take it so far that I would die. He beat the shit out of me for so long that I didn't even have the energy to dissociate, I felt it all.

He crouched down beside me when he finally stopped. 'You disgust me,' he said, as the blood and tears and snot dripped out of me. 'You absolutely disgust me. Listen – you are mine, you belong to me, and you will never, ever leave this house unless I say you can. Can you get that through your thick skull, bitch?' I nodded, unable to open my eyes fully, squinting at him through the swelling. 'Oh Christ, look at you. Get some fucking respect, get your life together, Scarlett. I'll always be here, always watching you – and if I'm not, I have plenty of people who will. You have anything to do for the kid, you do it during the day. If I catch you out this house after half past three, I'll fucking kill you.'

I believed him.

'I won't, Ed, I won't. I'll be good, I promise.'

He spat on my face, distorting his face in revulsion.

'I don't think you've got it in you. You better do as I say, but I think you won't be able to resist going out there, whoring around, making a fucking fool out of me. But remember – I can break every bone in your body, I can do whatever I want. And do you really think anyone would care? Do you really think anyone would even find you unless I wanted them to? I'll get rid of you and I'll take the boy. He'll never even know you existed. Is that what you want, Scarlett? Is it?'

I was shaking as I whimpered, 'No, no, please no.'

'Then we understand each other? You do everything I say – not what I ask. I won't be asking a slapper like you. You stop fucking every man on Regent Street unless I tell you to. And you stay in the house, you stay in the house that I provided for you.'

He kicked me again for good measure and left. And, as I lay there, all I could think was, *how do I make him love me now?*

Oh Scarlett, Scarlett. You're a mum now, but you're still that little girl craving love. You have

taken all he has thrown at you for three years, you have done everything you could – and he will never love you. You just can't see that you are nothing to him, but that desperate need which was fostered in you as a child still drives you, still rules over you. You are worth so much more than this. Every woman who lives this sort of life – and there are so many, so very many – thinks it is the only way to be. She thinks that there will be a miracle, that one day she will stop doing the things that make her abuser act this way, that she will be the woman he needs – that she will be a good girl. He doesn't want that, he doesn't even want you, he just wants a receptacle for other men to borrow while he struts around. Men like that will never change but women always hope they will. What will it take, Scarlett, what will it take?

Chapter Ten

My life

The violence became a regular occurrence – it was as if once Ed started something, once he had broken me down, that just became part of what happened between us. He was very good at it – after that first time, when he was in a frenzy, he tended to hit me on the head where my hair would cover any injuries, where bruises would go under my clothes, all the places you wouldn't see the consequences of his violence it if you walked past me in the street. It wasn't even for any reason, it was just because he felt like it.

One Saturday afternoon, Louise rang me.

'Is Danny at your Mum's?' she asked. He was. I'd dropped him off that morning so that my sister could spend some time with him there while I got the house cleaned. 'Fancy going into town for a bit?' I was keen to get out and buy a few bits for Danny. It was only just after lunchtime, so plenty of time to get back for my 3.30pm curfew, which I always stuck to. Another friend called Kirstin was waiting for me too when I got into town and we decided to have a couple of drinks before we popped to the shops. We were still young and always skint (me even more than them as I depended totally on Ed whereas they worked), so we got a big bottle of cider and went to sit in the churchyard. It was only 2pm when we got there, so I was good for curfew, and I had such a nice time. Of course, I made out that everything was great with Ed but Louise had witnessed how I lived on many visits to the house, so I doubt she was fooled.

I looked at my watch. It was half past four.

'Fuck! I need to get home,' I said to Lou and Kirstin. I rushed off on my own, walking as fast as I could and just praying that Ed hadn't come to the house in the last hour to see if I was there. I was heading towards the square in Wellington as I saw him coming round the corner. I don't know whether he had been to the house and was looking for me, or whether he was just out, but it didn't matter.

As soon as he clocked me, I knew what was coming. He'd drag me back home and knock seven shades out of me as usual. However, the closer he got the more I thought he couldn't even wait that long. He had that look on his face, the veil of anger and hatred which came over him whenever he was going to lay into me.

On each side of the square were shops, and one of them was a shoe shop with rails outside and running into the doorway holding boots, shoes, slippers, everything they sold. I went over, thinking I could hide until Ed passed, and bent over the racks. I knew he'd seen me and I knew it was inevitable, so when he grabbed me by the hair and dragged me out onto the street, there was pain but no surprise. It was Saturday afternoon and there were so many people out and about, all of them watching. I was sobbing, knowing the beating which was coming my way. He was swearing and throwing names at me the whole time, all the usual ones, and in an area like that, which was predominantly Pakistani, no one would have batted an eyelid at the insults. The place was mobbed, men, women, kids, all of them watching, most of them stopping to see what was going on, and no one doing a single thing.

He pulled me through the entrance to the street market, then through an alley to a car park. Unloading a van was the man who owned the fruit and veg stall in the market – he was also Pakistani – who stood and watched the entire beating I was given as if it was a sideshow. With a last kick at me, Ed screamed, 'I told you to stay at home, you fucking slag! You've got five minutes to get back there or you'll never walk again!' The fruit and veg man walked off, no doubt disappointed that the entertainment was over. I was in agony but I ran like I'd never run before.

I never went out again after half past three, and I never saw Louise or Kirstin again. It turned out that they were found that night by Ed and his friend, taken to the train bridge and hung over the sides, while told that their bodies would be found there if they ever spoke to me again.

I knew there was no way out now, this was my life. He had taken his anger out on me in a public place and no one had batted an eyelid, this was another level of control. I still get so angry about a community that can stand by and watch something like that, never mind knowing what is going on in the houses next door to them. If Ed could get away with that in front of over a hundred people, he was untouchable. I gave up, what was the point? He had broken me.

My entire 'relationship' with Ed was now violence and sex. He barely looked at Danny and I was relying more and more on Mum to keep my little boy safe from what was happening. I didn't think that Ed would hit Danny, but there was always the chance he could get caught in the cross-fire or, as he was getting older, witness what was going on so often. Ed wasn't there every night; sometimes I would just see him for a few moments as he popped in to check I hadn't broken curfew, but I was getting another very regular visitor.

Asad.

I never knew whether his father did actually own the house, but he certainly used it as a weapon for threats. I knew now that he could speak English, although not terribly well as he hadn't been born in the UK, but he certainly had an excellent use of the usual *slag, slut, whore* mantra. The first time he appeared without Ed, I simply told him he'd have to look elsewhere.

'No, am here for you. Am here for sorting out,' he told me, pushing his way in.

'No!' I said. 'Absolutely not.'

'Yes, sort me out,' he replied.

Horrified, I tried to shove him towards the door. 'I don't have to do anything with you if Ed isn't here. Fuck off.'

He considered this for a moment. 'I must ask Ed? I must ask Ed if I can fuck you?'

'It's nothing to do with Ed!' I shouted.

'So – when you sort me out, you want to sort me out? Is nice thing?' he asked. 'So, sort me out if Ed OK.'

We both knew that it was entirely up to Ed. I was completely under his control. Of course I didn't enjoy it, and I couldn't imagine how Asad could ever think that. 'I'm not doing it, I hate it and I am *not* doing it.'

'I think you maybe are,' he laughed. 'My house. My family's house. You fuck me or you go.'

And with that, he played his trump card. I was back to being raped on the sofa, on my own bed, on the floor, wherever yet another man wanted it. His rough hands all over me, his filthy dick in my mouth disgusting me as he pushed and pushed as far as he could go, ignoring my gagging, and the all-too-familiar motion of him thrusting and thrusting into my dissociated body. My white cottage was being visited on an almost daily basis between him and Ed.

I should have known it would accelerate – it always did. The day that Asad turned up at my door with two other men was one that I can hardly bear to even remember. He had been given a key by Ed after I had started locking both front and back and leaving keys in those locks. I was upstairs, having just put Danny to bed, when I heard the door open. I knew it would be him or Ed, and I resigned myself to what I'd have to get through, just hoping I wouldn't get battered into the bargain.

But I could hear laughing and I could hear more than one voice. As I went into the living room, Asad roared, 'here she is, here is our Scarlett. Just you wait,' he told the other two men, 'she will not disappoint!' They all laughed and spoke in Urdu, watching me. I knew enough of the language by now to understand that none of their words were anything other than sickening.

'First! I will be first!' Asad declared, and the other two patted him on the back as he passed them, pushing me out of the room and upstairs.

I lay on the bed that night and wanted to die. Asad then the other two, much older, men did whatever they liked with me, queuing up to have their turn. I doubt they even really thought of me as human. It was just something for them to do, and I was white trash so why would they think of me as a real person?

'It is good,' said Asad when he put his head round the door after the last one was finished with me. I tried to pull a sheet up over my body, but what was the point? They had seen everything and they had done everything. 'You are a good whore. I will be back.'

I lost count of how many more he brought. I knew in my heart of hearts that Ed was aware what was going on, but it was only later that I realised he was probably being paid for me. I have no doubt that he was pimping me out, while I didn't even get a penny for being prostituted. Asad even brought a really old man to me one day, claiming it was his cousin.

'On holiday,' he said. 'Sort out. Fuck him.'

The old man had two sticks and could barely walk. There was barely a tooth in his head and saliva was dribbling down his chin. He and Asad laughed together, with Asad having to shout to be heard, and then I was left in the living room with him. He wouldn't have been able to climb the stairs to my room.

I waited for him to take his clothes off, but Asad shouted through the door to me. 'Just suck. Just sort out that way. Too old.'

With the old man sitting on a chair in my front room, I felt vomit rise in my throat about what I was going to have to do. None of the men, apart from Ed, were ever clean, but this one smelled of death. There was something seeping from his pores that made me gag even before I was kneeling down in front of him. His eyes were rheumy behind his thick glasses and I wondered how long it had been since he had ever had sex. I know now that it probably wasn't that long ago at all. There was a conveyor belt of teenage white girls in Telford to do this, as I later found out.

It seemed to take forever, but when he was finally finished, I ran out of the room to be sick and brush my teeth. I didn't hear them leave, I had my head down the toilet and was crying my heart out. This was my life now.

There was another, equally old man, another alleged cousin, and I just couldn't do it. I tried to refuse but Asad threatened me again with the loss of the house.

'You fuck him or you leave.'

That was always the deal.

There were men in and out of the house all the time. He seemed to know when Ed wouldn't be there for a while or if he was away on one of the vague 'trips' he now spoke of, claiming that he had been charged to look out for me and check up on my behaviour. He said that Ed would kill me if I ever ran away, and that he would be happy to do that for him.

'I'm looking after you really, for Ed,' he would claim.

One night, he brought a new lad. This one, Haj, actually introduced himself to me and called me by my name. That was incredibly unusual as I was nothing more than a piece of meat to them. He didn't sneer or look disgusted at me. He seemed to think I was a normal girl and he didn't hurt me while he raped me. It wasn't as bad as the others and I tended to be grateful when it was him who arrived – that's how low the bar was.

I was letting Mum look after Danny more and more, because curfew time usually meant men 'visiting'. I never thought I would rely on her, but if he was at nursery or with me during the day, then she could pick him up when my 3.30pm deadline kicked in, I could make sure he was in bed when men came at night. One morning while Danny was at daycare, Asad came to mine for only a moment to tell me I had to meet him in thirty minutes at a house nearby.

'Be nice,' he said, 'be clean.'

That was a fucking joke; this lot were filthy bastards to a man. Urban Gardens was close to Regent Street. When I got there, he took me into the kitchen where there were loads of men sitting around. I genuinely didn't know how many, but definitely double figures. They were laughing and talking to each other in Urdu and I recognised the usual phrases of 'white slag, white whore'. I was a prostitute, I was filthy, but it didn't bother me anymore because I was everything they were calling me, wasn't I?

One man, who seemed to be about 40, took my arm and dragged me into the next room. It only had a mattress on the floor. He smiled and gestured at me to get undressed. I did and the inevitable happened, a searing pain ripping through me at the speed of his penetration which happened as soon as I lay down. He didn't use a condom, none of them ever did, and I wondered if they thought they were invincible in that department too. The mattress was stinking. I guess there had been plenty of girls like me on it in the past, and as I thought of that, another man came in.

'I will fuck you now too,' he told me.

And he did.

As did the next.

And the next.

As they all did – every man who was in that kitchen came up to that filthy mattress and raped me. Pain seared through my body and I honestly thought they must have damaged me beyond repair. I was allowed to get dressed and it hit me that I had to get back home quickly because my curfew was almost here. It hadn't saved me, it had happened at the time when I thought I would be OK at home, and now I was worried Ed would beat me for being out getting raped after 3.30pm.

I went back out through the same room they were all in, and they chanted and swore at me in Urdu as I walked past, calling me a filthy bastard, saying that I was disgusting. I agreed. I was. They had made me that way.

All of the houses I had ever been taken to – and there were plenty – looked the same inside. There was nothing homely in them, they were just dark, dingy, filthy shells with the bare minimum. One thing they all did have, though, was a mattress, always a double and always on the floor. These were nothing more than rape rooms. Kept for the sole purpose of taking girls like me, girls who meant nothing. White trash. Sometimes it would be strangers waiting for me, and sometimes men I had been given to on other occasions. There would be some who I saw quite often with their wives out and about, good family men, pillars of the community. They were always quick, it was always about them getting off, and there was never any conversation apart from the insults.

I knew that everyone on those streets must know about me. The men certainly did. One night, Ed's youngest brother came round and was so kind to me. It was the first time I could remember someone talking to me as a person in weeks. He kept saying, 'You need to get out, Scarlett. Stop doing it.' As if I had a choice! Next day he was beaten up and told never to see me again. I was poison – to myself more than anyone.

Time passed and I was taken to houses in Regent Street, Hadley and Leegomery and all of the places surrounding them. Everyone called me a slag so I believed that's what I was. All the white girls used to chase me, if they saw me, calling me a Paki shagger, telling me they would kill me for what I was doing, for what I was up to. I lived in constant fear. I needed out of the house, but the streets weren't safe either. Everywhere I went I was terrified. I didn't know which was worse – these girls catching me and beating me up, or meeting Ed, or Asad, or any one of the other men, and being raped.

And all the time I stayed. All the time I stayed there for Ed. Why? I knew that if I didn't, I would get beaten. I wasn't safe in my house and had never felt I was. I wasn't safe walking the streets as everyone hated me and wanted to show that through violence too, but the main reason was something else, something even more shameful. It was hope. When Ed was nice, it was everything. As much as that wasn't often, the nice times made me crave him more. I had been programmed to believe I was only alive for sexual reasons so having sex with these men was what I was supposed to do. I didn't know it was wrong, I didn't even know that I was being raped. I hadn't even known I was a victim when I was eight. Every single man I met raped or abused me in some way. That is what men did and I did what I had to do to survive. So, those moments when Ed smiled at me, or I watched him play with Danny, they were like a drug to me.

He took me to be raped at the back of the Telford United football ground and that hurt more than normal – as well as the actual sex ripping into me, it was on ground that was like a thousand cuts when it happened, cuts which reminded me for days afterwards. But he patted me on the arm afterwards and said, 'good girl, Scarlett, good girl.'

He took me to the Wrekin where we walked up a footpath a little as we chatted, stopped at a picnic spot and waited for two men to come and rape me while Ed went a little further away to have a cigarette. But we'd had that chat on the way there, and that was normal, that was lovely.

We went to another spot at the Wrekin where the Scouts used to meet and Ed signalled for two men as they approached. They said something in Urdu to each other while I stood shivering with fear. I was pushed over one of the trees which were laid down like long benches and raped by both of them from behind. But on the way back, Ed let me sit in the front of the car and bought me chips to take home.

I would take any scrap from him and he knew it.

There was no escape from the abuse and violence because everyone knew who I was and they were right in what they said I was – easy. If it was only one person I had to fight then it might have been easier to escape but it was everybody, it was a whole community. Ed was friends with everyone and he had told them all what a dirty slag I was, so they all thought I was fair game. He'd beat me for saying I didn't want to have sex with someone, he beat me for having sex with someone. I felt like he would actually beat me for simply breathing at the wrong time.

As time went on, I noticed that most of the men brought to me, or who I was taken to, were older, usually in their 50s. They all wore very traditional clothes and none of them spoke to me unless commanding me to do something – they'd worked out the English for that. They were usually in groups of three and they'd wait until one was done before they took their turn. It was so mechanical and I wondered what they were getting out of it too. I was still just a hole to them, and they were getting that, but I was starting to see that their treatment of me, the insults and the fact that I was a slave to them, must have been part of what they got off on too.

At home, I knew now to keep the door unlocked; I'd get battered if I didn't. I was now at the stage where I would sit in my living room, just waiting. They'd just walk in. I knew I had to go upstairs, while the rest of the group would wait downstairs and then swap. They were all smelly, a mixed stench of body odour and curry. I can't stand the smell of strong garlic to this day.

I was just a receptacle for them. I never got a penny from any of those men but Ed would constantly tell me how lucky I was, living on his money. He would check up on me every day, any time – there was no curfew now, I had to be available 24 hours a day, 7 days a week. Sometimes Ed would play with Danny while these men did horrible things to me. The doting father. He'd beat me for a speck of dust on a skirting board or if I looked at him the wrong way. I was nothing. I accepted it all. Still only 17, and I had no way out.

I know you feel helpless and completely trapped right now, Scarlett. If you don't do what you're told you don't know whether you are going to be kicked out onto the streets with nowhere to live or found dead in a gutter. You are so scared about what they will do with Danny – would Ed actually look after your boy if he killed you? Or would he suffer the same fate? Keep going, they can't take away what's inside of you. They can rape and beat you, they can humiliate and abuse you, but they will never take away your fighting spirit. Hold on – you're simply doing what you have to do to survive and in that there is no shame. They are the ones who will have to answer for this, not you. They are the ones who are making a mockery of the faith they claim to have, the code they claim to live by. They are the ones who will, one day, be scared of you and what you will achieve.

Chapter Eleven

Just a girl

He's fucking around. I just knew it. *He's cheating.*

I bet that is no surprise to anyone reading this. How could this man even be expected to stay faithful to me when he was treating me appallingly? He was hardly some romantic lover, but there was something that hit me when I was almost 18 and made me finally open my eyes.

There was one girl on our street who obviously hated me. Whenever I was out with Danny, Gillian would look daggers at me, shout out that I was a disease-ridden slut, a disgrace. When I was in the car with Ed, if she ever walked by, he would smile and wave at her. It was her, I just knew it.

On the street one day, after drinking a bit that morning, I plucked up the courage to confront her. Shouting names over, she flew at me as I called to her that I wanted a fight. I was losing it completely, wanting to be violent to her, wanting to take it out on her.

'What you so stressed about, Scarlett?' she asked.

'You! I'm stressed about you!'

'What the hell do you think I've done?'

'You call me names all the time . . .'

'What? Like you've just done to me?'

'Well, I've got good reason.'

'Really? Go on, then, tell me,' she mocked.

'You're fucking Ed. You're cheating with my boyfriend! You're his other girlfriend!'

She laughed in my face. 'His girlfriend? Love, I couldn't even *count* how many girlfriends he's got, but I'm not one of them. He fucks me sometimes, but he does that with everyone,' she shrugged. 'You need to see him for what he is, Scarlett. Yeah, he's a good-looking lad, but he treats you like shit, everyone knows that.'

'So why does everyone else treat me like that too? Why were you shouting names at me?'

Gillian thought about it for a moment then smiled. 'You know what? I don't even know. We just do, don't we? They call us all that stuff, and we do it to each other. Maybe it makes us feel better? If you're a slag, then I'm not. If it's always someone, then does it matter?'

We became quite good friends after that. Gillian would come over to the house, we'd have a drink together, and I really liked having someone around since Louise had been frightened off – but Ed found out. He found everything out. He'd batter me for talking to her and batter her for talking to me.

'We need to get away for a bit,' she said one day. 'I'm sick of this.'

'Ed would never let us!'

'Don't tell him. Give the kid to your mum and we can go see my family. We can go for a week, Scarlett, we can go for two weeks!' I was terrified but I did it. The morning we left, I sneaked out of the house, finally feeling that I would have some fun in my life. I'd pay for it when I got back, but that would be something I would have to deal with when it happened.

It was just what I needed. I just wanted to forget everything back in Telford. We drank, took drugs, smoked constantly, but I also spent the first week gradually forgetting what my other life was like. I had a fake ID that Gillian had got for me, so we could get into any pub or club, and I managed to fit in all the years I had missed into those seven days.

'I've got a mate we should go see,' Gillian shouted to me one night, over the blaring music in the club.

My heart sank and she must have seen the look in my eyes.

'No, no! Not a mate like Ed's mates. A real one – he's got a barge! Want to go stay on a barge for a night or two?'

I did. I wanted to try and do everything! I'd never had a real holiday before, and this was something that could take me out of all of the things I knew would be there when I got back.

We got onto the barge the next day and although it wasn't the prettiest thing I had ever seen, I was delighted to have the experience. Gillian's friend, George, was old and scruffy. He seemed happy to have us there and was obviously close to Gillian. He poured us both a drink . . . and that was the last thing I remembered. I did groggily sort of come to every now and again, but couldn't walk, couldn't talk. I just lay on this long, padded seat and waited. I would have wondered what the hell I had got myself into now but wasn't even capable of doing that.

I started to become aware of the barge's movements. We seemed to stop quite a lot, never really going along the canal ways for long before I would hear Gillian and George get off the deck. I would fall back into drugged slumber for a while, then hear them come back. On the occasions when I managed to open my eyes, I would see that the barge would be full of things like TVs and electrical gadgets after every stop. They were clearly robbing houses along the way and keeping me quiet as they did so – I have no idea whether George was doing anything else to me while I was in that state too. After a few days, I came to.

'You're back with us!' Gillian cried, as if she hadn't had anything to do with it.

'You should come and meet my girls,' the old man told me. 'Come on, up you get.' He was a pimp. Just like all the others. He took us to one house after another where he seemed to keep very young girls, younger than me, in conditions that looked just like all the houses I had been taken to over the past three years. Gillian seemed perfectly comfortable there and chatted to them all – I was horrified. No way was I getting into this. It was just the same situation but without Danny.

When we got back, Ed was waiting for me, parked outside the house, not inside it, and I assumed that he had been there every day. It was a beating like no other I had ever had. The blows rained down on me – as they always did. He seemed like a man possessed – as he always did. My body was aching, screaming out for mercy – as it always did.

I knew there was nothing I could do to stop this. He was the one who chose when it happened, and all I could do was wait it out. I was only a teenager and yet this was my life. It had been my life for so long and I had never been able to choose. I went from beating to beating, kicked and punched, used and abused. When it wasn't happening, I was living in fear of it happening and of how much it would hurt. That pain and that fear coloured every moment of my life.

'You whore! How dare you act like this?' he screamed at me. 'How dare you not do what I say? How dare you think you have any say in this! How dare you show me up in front of my friends! Whore, whore, whore!'

He had obviously still been bringing men round to be 'sorted out' while I was away and, for him, the most awful thing was that I hadn't been there to service them. He hadn't been able to provide the goods that he was known for – and no doubt being paid for, and I was the one responsible for that. I could actually see his argument. I was so conditioned, so locked into the horror he had created, that I wasn't surprised in the slightest.

Whatever I was, he had made me that way. I did everything for him, no matter how disgusting, no matter how degrading. I could never anticipate whether those things would be the right ones, but even in the few moments when he treated me as a human being, I knew it would always revert to this. I would dance to his every command, my broken body just a vessel for him to use. He didn't see me as a person, as a woman, I was just a thing. A thing that he despised but who he kept in his life because she could sometimes be of use to him. And all the time I hoped for a glimmer of something – not love, that would be too much to hope for, but maybe something close to humanity.

'You are nothing!' Ed screamed at me. 'Nothing!' his face contorted with anger and hatred as he continued to kick and punch my wretched body. 'Do you hear me? Do you hear me? You are worthless. You are less than the dirt on my shoes. You will never EVER leave this house again unless you ask for my permission. You have been told this so many fucking times, Scarlett – why do you do this? Why do you bring this on yourself?'

'Please, Ed, please . . .' I wept.

'Shut up! Shut up!' he yelled back. Then he stopped. He finally stopped. Crouching down beside me on the filthy floor, he held my face in his hand. A jaw long broken. A nose that had gone the same way. Bruises and cuts and welts.

'You disgust me,' he hissed. 'You are nothing, do you understand? You are nothing. You – you are just a girl, a stupid whore of a girl.'

With that, he let my face drop from his hands and walked out of the room, slamming the door behind him. Every part of me ached, but it was my heart that felt it most. This shouldn't be my life, this shouldn't be anyone's life. His words rattled around in my head – *just a girl, just a girl*. That's all I had ever been to men, wasn't it? From my father onwards, I was nothing more. I was only there to be something for them to inflict pain upon.

I knew that wouldn't be the last time I would be kicked like an animal, but I truly believe that it was the moment when something changed in my mind. Perhaps it was overload. Perhaps my body had taken so much that, subconsciously, a little voice had said to me, *just get out alive – get out alive and you can do anything.*

I dragged myself up, feeling blood drip down my face from a gash at the side of my head, old and new bruises mingling together and creating a pulse throughout every inch of my body. I was filthy, aching from it all, terrified of more days and nights like these. But I'd heard that voice for the first time. It wasn't telling me I was worthless or a whore. It wasn't telling me that this would never change. It had finally woken up. I wasn't out, but I knew this couldn't go on forever. I'd be killed one way or another, either by Ed or by taking my own life.

He was invincible. If he ever saw me outside the house, even when I'd got permission to go for something like nappies, he would spit on me in front of people. He'd tell me to get home or he'd kill me, and onlookers would either say nothing, or, sometimes, if they were men like him, they'd laugh. His cars were getting bigger and bigger, I knew he'd moved in a beautiful new house of his own, and yet I was the one making money for him on my back or on my knees. On one occasion, he told me to pick up money for him from a flat in Wellington. He warned me not to look in the envelope and not to even think of taking any of it, because I deserved nothing.

When I got there, there were three men – and I knew what was coming before they even started. A huge fat guy pushed me into a back room, so deserted that there wasn't even a mattress. He raped me with such force and such hatred that I felt he was taking out on me what he must have been holding inside for the first woman he had a chance to attack. He gave me a kick as he left the room, crossing paths with the second man who did the same to me. The first one had hurt me so much that I was bleeding, and the gratitude I felt when the third one didn't come through was enormous – but appalling when you think about it. I'd only been raped by two, not three; what a blessing. They gave me the money and I trotted obediently back to Ed's car which was waiting round the corner.

'You took your fucking time,' he said. 'Enjoying yourself, were you?' I lay in the back, crying silent tears, terrified that the blood pouring from me might stain his seats.

I'd gone out one day with Danny in his pushchair to drop him off with Mum, when Ed saw us. I had been put straight back into being pimped out for all the men he knew, but I was hoping that the little voice would come back and help me shout loud enough to make him hear and make him see I couldn't go on.

'Oi, you,' he shouted, getting out of the car. 'Come with me, get down the back of these fucking garages.'

'No,' I said. I had Danny with me and no way was I risking there being someone there I had to 'meet' or getting a kicking from Ed while my little boy was watching. I knew I'd done something to make him angry but I'd no idea what it was.

'Get here now!' He stomped over to me, grabbed the pushchair, and tipped it upside down with Danny still in it. I was screaming as Ed dragged the buggy with a crying Danny behind the garages so I had to follow. He punched me in the face and split my nose instantly. I fell into a bush, and still had no idea what I had done. But I did know I'd had enough. My baby was in danger now, and I couldn't stand for that. I stood up as Ed went to storm off.

'I hate you, you black bastard!' I shouted.

'What did you say?' he retorted, coming back. 'Want to say it again, white slag? Go on, try it.' He came back and punched me in the face, right on my split nose. I shouted the same again as he walked off. He came back, punched me again, walked off and I whispered it, desperately needing the last word. I had a split nose and two black eyes from that – and it was worth it.

I went to the council offices the very next day and said that my landlord was kicking me out. I'm not sure if it was looking at my face that did it, but they put me in a hostel that same day for 6 weeks. It was grim but at least I was out of it – or so I thought.

Not long after I moved into the hostel, another set of Pakistani lads started hanging around. They had been friends with Ed but they'd all fallen out for some reason or other. The room I had been given was on the ground floor and they seemed to know I was there almost from the start. They'd hammer on the bay windows after 5pm, when the staff left for the day, telling me to open them. I didn't for a while, but they were actually nice and just used to chat to me through the opened window, asking me how I was and badmouthing Ed. After a while, I trusted them, so would open the window and let them in. I was desperate for some company and, to be honest, glad that someone else didn't like Ed either. There were three different lads, but only one or two would come to the hostel at a time, so it was nice to have that sort of contact. They were my friends. They'd chat and never tried to have sex, which was all I wanted really.

I was closer to one of them – Faisal – than the others as he seemed more sympathetic. One night he said, 'Why don't you get a babysitter tomorrow afternoon, Scarlett? We can go out, have a bit of a laugh?' It was just what I needed. The girls in the hostel all helped each other out, and there was no difficulty in finding someone to take care of Danny. All I wanted was a drink and a few hours away from everything at a normal, local pub.

Faisal picked me up next day in his car. 'Where do you fancy going?' I asked him.

'Don't you worry,' he said. 'I've got a little place in mind.' I should have known there was no pub. He took me to a house nearby, just like all the others, where there were three of his cousins who were visiting from Birmingham he claimed. They were all sitting around, smoking draw and drinking. Good Muslims. I had a few drinks too as they were actually perfectly nice to me even though I had a sinking feeling in the pit of my stomach, but they must have put something in it. I have no idea what happened, but I woke up in a bed with all three of them laughing at how I'd did it with them all. 'You liked that! Yes, you had fun! Did you like all of that in you, filthy slut?' All of their voices were as one, all of them feeling so pleased with what they did to me. I'm sure I wasn't the first, nor would I be the last.

'You are right!' one of them laughed to Faisal. 'She will do anything!' Faisal dropped me back at the hostel and I never saw him, or the other two who had visited me, again.

After six weeks, I was moved out of the hostel into my own house. It wasn't in a Pakistani area and I felt that gave me breathing space – at last I was out. Everything was second-hand – or third, or fourth – and, honestly, it was a shit tip, but it was my shit tip. I cleaned it from top to bottom, begged everyone I knew for little bits to make it homely, and honestly thought things might turn out better until I realised that I hadn't had my period that month. As soon as the thought came into my head, I realised I had a funny taste in my mouth, I'd been feeling a bit sick, all of the symptoms I'd had with Danny.

This time, I knew I didn't want it. The father could only be one of the men from the rape in that house while I lived in the hostel, and there was no way I was having a child conceived under those circumstances. I told my GP that I had been raped – which was the truth – and no more questions were asked. I was given a date and knew that I would follow through this time. If there was anything that could make it worse, it was the reappearance of Ed. Someone in the area I now lived knew him and had reported that I was there. He hammered on the door the very afternoon I got back from the GP, shell-shocked but ready to do what I had to do.

'That was some fucking number you did on me!' he roared. 'Disappearing, taking my kid. You really think you could get away with that, Scarlett?'

I was exhausted. 'Oh, fuck off, Ed. Shout at me, kick me, do you what you like. I'm done. And I'm pregnant.'

'How pregnant? Is it mine? I've not fucked you in months, I'm disgusted by you whoring your way around Telford.'

'No, it's not yours.'

'Well, you're not having a kid who isn't mine. You're getting an abortion this time, you hear me?'

'I'm way ahead of you there,' I told him. 'It's all sorted.' He told me that he would take me to the clinic, 'to make sure,' but I was never going to change my mind on this. Those disgusting men had done enough to me; I wouldn't let them do this as well.

I'd never had an operation before and was absolutely terrified. All I remember was the mask going over my face then waking up again. The staff asked if I had a lift arranged, and I told them that Ed would be back for me at 2pm. 2pm came and there was no sign of him. 3pm came and there was no sign of him. 4pm came and there was no sign of him. The nurses were getting annoyed at me so I said that he was outside and they let me go. I knew he wouldn't be turning up, he'd let me down as he always did. The painkillers were wearing off, and I had no money, but I walked to the train station and just hoped no one would ask to see a ticket at either end. Tired, drained, bleeding, the only person I could think to call was Louise's mum. I reversed the charges and told her I was at the station, that I'd had an abortion a couple of hours ago, and I wasn't feeling too well.

'Don't move,' she said. 'I'll be there in five minutes.'

True to her word, I'd never been more relieved to see anyone in my life. She took me to her house and I stayed overnight – truth be told, I wanted to stay there forever, I'd always loved the house and the feeling of safety in it.

Once I was feeling better, I never looked back from the abortion. I decided that, if I was to turn my life around, I needed to go back to education.

I'd need help, so, reluctantly, I went to see Mum. 'I want to go to college, and study business. Danny can go to the creche, and I might be able to make something of myself at last,' I said, expecting laughter at the very least, but she surprised me. 'Would you maybe be able to collect him a couple of times a week?'

'I'll do whatever I can to support you, Scarlett. I know it hasn't been easy with that boy. He might be Danny's father, but he's no good for you. You need to live a little, you really do. Go to college. Danny can stay here Monday to Friday and you can take over on weekends. No need to put him in with strangers – leave him with someone who loves him.' I couldn't believe it. She was finally stepping up to the plate, finally helping me.

It wasn't easy to get a place at college, but there were kind people who helped me, and I felt my future was getting sorted. *It'll all be good*, I would tell myself, a mantra that kept me going. I would spend my day at college, study when I got home, I was even thinking of getting a little part-time job. Of course, I was missing Danny terribly but Mum was doing well, in her own way. When I picked up my two-year-old every Friday, she was a bit dramatic, clinging on to him and wailing, 'oh, please let it be Monday soon!' but I'd just roll my eyes and head home with my son. At the other end of the week, I would be counting the days to Friday.

On one of those Mondays with the whole week stretched out in front of me without Danny, I had a half day from college to catch up on some studies. I'd just made myself a cup of tea and settled down with my books when there was a knock at the door.

A bloke I didn't recognise was standing there.

'Scarlett Jones?' he asked. I nodded. 'Here you go,' he said, passing me an envelope before leaving without another word.

It was a court summons.

It had been less than two months but she couldn't wait. Mum wanted custody of Danny. She'd been playing the long game all along.

Scarlett, I want to tell you that you are so, so desperate to be loved, to feel that kind of love that normal people have, that you are accepting far, far less than you deserve. You aren't what they tell you. You are beautiful inside and out, you were a child that had her childhood taken away from her and you've lost all of that time since. You're trying, you've made the first steps, and, although you keep getting dragged back in, there's no disgrace in that. Anyone who has been groomed the way you have been is adrift, a lost soul. There are those who would give you meaningless words, they would tell you that the answer has been in you the whole time or that we make our own destiny – that may very well be true when you are an adult with a world of resources at your feet, but it is an insult to apply it to a raped child or a trafficked girl. You are in this through no fault of your own and the fates seem to be against you at every turn. All I can do is watch, and weep a little for the Scarlett who was, and wait. I'll wait for you.

Chapter Twelve

This is who you are

When it got to court, key statements came from Mum's health visitor friends. I wasn't even allowed to speak – but I was speechless anyway when I saw who was standing beside her. Ed. They'd teamed up to take Danny away from me. I was lost, I didn't know the process but they all seemed confident. The Judge told me to be quiet every time I tried to speak as it always seemed to be at the wrong time. It was said that I was a druggie, a prostitute, and Ed confirmed it all. He said that he was terrified for his son's welfare and that he feared there would be no future for his beloved boy if left with me. He said that he was a good man, a hard worker, and just wanted someone to give him a chance to save his son.

She got him.

Mum got Danny.

I could only see him every other weekend but, during those weekends, Ed was to have time with him which I was to facilitate. These meetings had to be at a contact centre so that the social workers could observe how Ed interacted with Danny, and the reports were glowing. They all commented on how there was such a bond and he was a fantastic father; no one listened to a word I said about what kind of man he really was.

I eventually got a solicitor and an injunction on Ed. He was still allowed sessions with Danny, but the solicitor agreed I shouldn't have to see my abuser every time there was a meeting. I was told I could drop Danny off and collect him without seeing Ed at all.

He wanted custody now and there were constant court meetings, where the main angle seemed to be that Danny needed his heritage. No one listened to me for months and it was breaking my heart. I turned up early one day to collect my little boy and waited in the car park, where he was usually brought to me.

I saw him walking out the door holding the hand of a man one day, with the handover social worker behind him.

'Do you know who the fuck that is?' I asked her, when the man had gone and I walked over to get my son.

'What do you mean?' she asked. 'It's his dad, of course.'

'Really?' I pressed. 'You sure of that are you?'

'Scarlett, I don't know what you're getting at but this isn't funny.'

'And he's doing well, is he? Great dad? Great bond with Danny? Turns up on time every session?'

'Yes,' she said. 'You know all of that, it's in the reports.'

'And you've done no fucking checks whatsoever, have you, because THAT is not ED, THAT is his fucking older brother who has been doing the contact sessions every two weeks!' It was a joke, but they always seemed to take the side of Mum and Ed. I never did get a satisfactory answer to the fact they hadn't even clocked the wrong person was coming, but I did go back to court and they had to admit Ed hadn't been attending. They took away his contact rights but Mum retained custody.

I'd given up college when I lost Danny. It had been six months of pretending that I was ever going to have a straightforward life, but I was now back to the world I knew of heartbreak and abuse. I was drinking a lot and spending most nights in the local pubs. One night, I met a lovely lad called Alan and we started seeing each other. I was his first girlfriend, and it was a completely normal relationship with no hitting, no nastiness whatsoever. However, what he didn't know was that Ed had started harassing me again (isn't it interesting the words we use to minimise the horrors of our lives?), and was coming to the house whenever he liked, having sex with me whenever he liked. He was still violent, but I convinced myself that it was a bonus not to have to fuck other men for him. Another part of my new normality was that I had a friend – a young girl called Shelley had moved in next door and we became close (we're still good friends to this day). She spent a lot of time in my house too. Ed still thought he was invincible and that women would never stand up to him, Shelley actually saw me fly off the back of the sofa when he punched me for absolutely nothing one afternoon. He was telling me at this point that he would kidnap Danny, take him to Pakistan and I'd never see him again. I honestly believed he would do that, especially since he was sticking to his threats that I'd be found dead in a ditch if he wanted that, or that I would simply disappear if he gave one of his 'boys' the signal.

On another occasion, he marched in the front door while I was on the toilet, punched me off the seat without a word, then walked back out. I wasn't even safe there. It was after that when I started to wonder about having something nearby for self-defence that would finally stop him in his tracks. Could I keep the chip pan on and throw the boiling oil in his face? I'd go to prison but I needed to think of ways to hurt or damage or maim or kill him. The other option was to tell the police, but would they actually do anything? Ed was untouchable and I didn't know if he had them in his pocket too. It was worth a try before I took any other approach, I thought. The next time he beat me, I called them. It was predictable when the officer said, 'I can't see anything – you sure this happened, love, or are you just a bit annoyed with him?'

'He does it in places you can't see – I'll have bruises all over tomorrow and I have wounds that will never heal. You could get my medical records, see how many times he's broken my nose and split my lip.'

'Sounds like a domestic to me,' he said, shrugging. 'What do you expect us to do?'

I tried again a few weeks later, and it was the same as it had been before, but with the added bonus of the policeman being an absolute scumbag too.

'Actually, you're a very pretty woman,' he leered. 'Why don't you come round and see me next week? I'll give you my address – if the curtains are open, it's fine, but if they're shut, the wife's there, so don't bother.' Of course, I never did but it reiterated that that was all men wanted me for. Even the police saw me as a slag. I must have tried to get them to help me properly about twenty times. They did speak to Ed but there were never any charges; I think he finally realised that I wouldn't stop so gave up for a while, although he continued to collude with Mum.

I'd been seeing Alan more often but honestly, it wasn't a big love story (although he was perfectly nice), I just wanted a baby. I quickly got pregnant again and it was definitely Alan's as Ed had disappeared after the police had spoken to him. Alan was so excited, it was how it should be.

Shelley, my next-door neighbour was pregnant too, and it was lovely to go through it together. This was who I was for about six months, and I loved it. Although I missed

Danny hugely, I hoped that I would be able to show I was a good mum with the new baby and get him back.

At my six months ante-natal check, the sonographer said to me, very casually, 'Want to know what kind you're having, Scarlett?' Alan was desperate to find out so we said, 'Yes please' and were told it was a little girl. We were both happy, but that night, something changed. I felt so uneasy as if something had been triggered.

The next day when Shelley came to my house, I was still unsettled and felt very emotional. We were playing a board game when I started crying uncontrollably.

'What's wrong, Scarlett? What's wrong?' said Shelley, instantly concerned. 'Are you bleeding? Do you have cramps?'

I shook my head.

'I'm having a girl,' I told her.

'Yes, I know! You told me yesterday! Are you just really happy, did you want a girl?'

How could I tell her? How could I tell her what I was really feeling? What I was terrified of? 'I don't know what to do, Shelley, I don't know if I can have a girl. I know what sort of world I'd be bringing her into and what that world does to girls.'

I told her everything about my dad that afternoon. Everything – and her response was very simple: 'You need to go to the police.' I knew she was right. I knew she was telling me what hit true in my heart and, the next day, I walked into my local police station and said that I needed to speak to someone. I was all over the place and my police experiences had been so bad up to that point, I thought they'd say I was crazy.

They didn't.

They arranged for me to speak with a specialist officer at Wellington police station, back to the same place as when I was 15 and Mark had drawn his pictures which had caused the last police involvement in our family. Thankfully, I got a female officer who was lovely to me. I told her everything about Dad and it took her hours to hand write it all. I could actually see tears in her eyes as she was writing it down. I said nothing about Ed though – after all, that was all my fault and I deserved it, whereas I was just a little girl when Dad abused me. She gave me a lift home and said they'd be in touch.

I knew I had to tell Mum. I wanted her to know and I wanted to see her reaction. Our relationship had always been so fractured but now she'd taken my son too and I almost wanted her to feel sorry for me and give him back.

Walking up to her door felt like the longest walk of my life. She opened it and stared at me.

'What do *you* want?' she said, with that lip curl she always had on her face when she spoke to me. 'You're not wanted here. Piss off.'

'I need to tell you something, Mum . . .' I began.

'Funny – there's nothing I want to hear from you.'

'You'll want to hear this. I've been to the police, Mum. I've told them about something I've carried for years.' I took a deep breath. 'Dad . . . Dad used to rape me when I was a little girl.'

She looked at me for two seconds tops, then slammed the door in my face. I was later told that she went straight in and phoned Dad, telling him that she needed to see him about 'an important matter.' She went to Blackpool where he was now living and stayed overnight with him in a hotel. He'd left her after he was accused of abusing a child. He was getting married to another woman. Her daughter had just said he raped her as a child. Why would you do that? Why would you go to a man like that?

Mum wasn't the only one who was deluded. A few days after I had reported Dad, I actually got an invitation to his wedding. As my RSVP I called his wife-to-be and told her I wouldn't be coming to the wedding.

'Why?' she asked me.

'Quite frankly, he's a rapist. Before you marry him, you need to know what he's really like. I've been to the police and they have taken all my evidence.'

'Why would you do that now?' she screamed. 'You've got over it, you're having another baby! Why would you ruin his life?'

'You have kids, you have to make a decision, and you have to protect them,' I pleaded.

'I have made my decision – I'm marrying him.' With that, she put the phone down.

I promised myself that I wouldn't let any of this spoil my pregnancy. I had been to the police, it was in their hands now, and when I gave birth to my beautiful Lola not long after I turned 19, I genuinely was instantly in love with her. Alan was by my side the whole time and it was a completely different experience to the time I had Danny, but I couldn't see it. Why didn't Alan hit me? Why didn't he treat me like filth? His family was great and they welcomed me with open arms as if they couldn't actually see what I was – I felt like it was only a matter of time. I was with Alan for ten years, but I always thought he would turn. I don't have a bad word to say about that man, but he paid the price for my past as much as I did.

A few months after Lola was born, the police got in touch to say that the Crown Prosecution Service had rejected my claim. It was my word against his. I was crying, the policewoman was crying too, saying she believed me, but I remembered what Dad had always told me: if I ever mentioned this to anyone, they'd say it was my fault. He'd been right all along, that's just how it felt.

The policewoman referred me to a woman who ran a sexual abuse victims group in a little church hall in Telford. I never fitted in, the rest weren't like me, and I could see everything that they were doing wrong – this wasn't the sort of service that was needed. However, it turned out that the woman in charge was ex-police who was able to get a copy of my files. I had all of my statements – but also all of Dad's. He'd been dragged out of bed at 6am and I liked that.

He had said to them, 'Yeah, I used to lie naked on the bed next to her. So what? If I want to have an erection on my own bed, it's her choice to look in and see it.'

He'd never denied or confirmed anything.

What many people don't realise is that the effects of sexual abuse don't stop when the abuse stops. When you have had that all through your childhood – and, for me, my teenage years too – it's hard to understand that you weren't just put here for sex. My relationship with Alan was too normal for me and I was rarely faithful to him over those ten years we were together. I had lived in a state of flight or fight for so long, but I didn't need it with him, so I craved danger. I'd always not known what was coming next, so now that I had normality, I was always in manic mode. It was all I'd known. If I went on a night out, I'd be drawn to the dangerous ones and I cheated on Alan so many times. That's just what I did – I was a slag. He knew but he loved me and accepted it which was worse.

Over those ten years I actively sought help, telling doctors I wanted to die and that I couldn't cope with what had happened to me. I was given tablets that made me feel weird and when I looked them up, they were for schizophrenia. I was furious. I went to see the GP the next day and said, 'I know what happened to me, and it was *to* me, not to some other personality I've invented. I need help, not some crap diagnosis so that you can tick a box.'

'What do you expect for people like you?' he asked, coldly. 'I don't have a magic pill so those are your only option. This is just who you are – it would be better if you accepted it.' I walked out crying. *People like me*. I was different, wasn't I? I was abnormal. So, as I always did, I decided to try and fake normal – this time, by having another baby. In 1990, when I was 20, we had Freddy. I was relieved that it was another boy. I loved Lola to bits but I was still terrified that she would suffer the same fate I had. Alan was a good man but there were so many out there who were not. I goaded him so much, tried to get reactions from him, tested the boundaries to see if he would hit me, go out knowing what I was doing to do. He let it all happen, he never reacted, he always walked away from it, until I ended it. He needed to be given that, he needed to have his life back.

Danny was becoming a hindrance to Mum as she was in a new relationship and he wasn't the cute little baby she had wanted. I still had fortnightly access, but she couldn't even let me have my own child when she was fed up of him and gave him to Jackie. I was devastated when I heard that my sister was joining in, but she only put up with him for two weeks and I got him back forever. It was a different relationship for us. I'd never been allowed to bond with Danny. A part of him blamed me for that but I finally had my family back, even though Danny and I never really had an easy time of it.

Even when Alan left, I was drinking. It's so wonderful to be able to escape your own memories, even for a little while, but they're back the next day as is the guilt that you're hurting the ones you love too. I wasn't good at relationships – I couldn't trust or understand them. I'd only known abuse and that's not normal. I was losing the plot. My depression was getting worse and suicidal thoughts were prevalent all the time – until fate stepped in. I met a bloke at work and had an affair for a few months, finding out I was pregnant on my 30th birthday.

I believe that baby was sent to save me. Without being pregnant with her, I wouldn't be here. I stopped drinking the moment I found out and decided again to try and sort myself out. Marnie was born at home with all of my other kids there too, cuddling her within seconds of her entrance into the world. It was something I'd never forget.

Since Danny's birth I'd used weight as a way of self-harming myself. If I was fat, no one would find me attractive, everyone would leave me alone – it wasn't true, as my behaviour had shown, but it was something I needed to tackle. When Marnie started school, I began to lose weight as I was happier in myself. I had a good group of friends and I wasn't drinking all the time. When I was big, there was a lad I'd always liked, probably for ten years or more. Jimmy never gave me the time of day. I hated that – all men wanted sex, so why not him? When I lost five stone, I went out one night and he finally spoke to me. We swapped numbers and started to meet up, but only at mine during the day as he worked nights.

After six months, I was pregnant again. By that time, Jackie and I had grown a lot closer and she was the first one I told. She was so happy for me and it seemed that things were finally coming together – for about a day. Jimmy, wonderful Jimmy, who I had wanted for so long, who had finally deigned to be with me, hadn't been working nights all along. He'd been at home, with his wife, with his other life. It was all a lie and I'd been pushed over again by yet another man. I still didn't want to give up on it, I still didn't want to give up on love.

Jackie was there when I gave birth to my baby boy, Max. Jimmy didn't come to the hospital, he didn't see his son until we got home, but he was quick enough to start having sex with me again as soon as he could. He was clear that he wouldn't leave his wife, but I was back to thinking I was a slag again, so why not?

This is what abuse does. It rips you up and makes you unable to see what is normal, what is right. When you have been so messed up as a child, so deliberately lied to and threatened, when you have been ripped to shreds emotionally, mentally and physically, how can you ever go into the next stage of your life thinking you're worth anything more than *that*? There is a walking army of us out there, but, when I was back in that part of my life, four kids and a world of pain, I would never have seen that there would soon be something that I had done, for me, which would bring me more pride and satisfaction than I had ever known.

I know that you have days where you want to end it all, where you don't want to wake up. I know you have sat in the bath and asked God, who you don't even know if you believe in, if He can help you die. I know how much you hurt from everything you've experienced, and how much it is affecting the life you thought you could have. Against all of the odds, you are here and I believe there must be a reason for that. We survivors don't have an easy or clear path once the pain is over – because it's only others who can ever think that the pain is truly *over. We'll always carry it, but we must reach a place where we carry it with stillness, in a place where we acknowledge it but come to terms with it. Remember, Scarlett, the only one who needs to be forgiven is you. You don't have to be the 'bigger' person, you don't have to forgive – but you need to find a way to build a life that isn't just an existence. Come on, Scarlett, come on.*

Chapter Thirteen

Justice

Jackie and I never really spoke to each other about the abuse but in 2012 she told me that, when I made my allegations, the police had asked her whether she could confirm what had happened to me – and she had denied it all. She now told me that, as I had suspected that day when I screamed at her, *is he doing this to you too?* that, yes, he had abused her for years too – as had our grandad. Did I want to go to the police with her? she asked. Yes. God, yes. I'd been waiting years for this. I'd been waiting on this for over thirty years and my life had been on pause until I was given permission to take this forward. I was ecstatic. I'd given up, but this gave me a flicker of hope. Maybe now that I had someone else on my side, the CPS would look favourably on it.

Jackie felt that she would be confident writing a letter, detailing all of her abuse, rather than visiting the police station. We got our first stroke of luck with that as it went to an officer who actually cared. He had seen she'd said in the letter that she didn't know what to do, but he knew. This officer was in charge of the Historical Abuse Unit (I hate that phrase as it implies that the abuse is over and done with) which was why he'd had it passed to him. This officer turned up at Jackie's and arranged for her to do a video interview, calling me afterwards and asking for me to give more video evidence. I didn't dare think that anything would happen, but what I dreaded was that I would do it and they'd say 'no further action'.

I was picked up by two officers called Cindy and Steve, never thinking for a moment that they would become like family. I'd always felt there was something wrong with me and I certainly didn't trust the police but they were so genuine, treating me as if I was normal – which I knew I wasn't.

In a deserted building in the middle of nowhere, I was taken to a very homely room with a camera in the corner. Cindy sat with me as Steve recorded, and I told her everything about Dad. Again. Over six hours, I was emotionless apart from the time I spoke about when he had anally raped me as I could still feel the pain in the memory. That broke me.

Other things came through to me. The time Mum was in London with the kids, after I had told her and she still left me with him. He put a pornographic film on and told me I had to watch it. I was so uncomfortable – this was real and different from the magazines. He paused the old VCR, went upstairs, bringing back suspenders and stockings which I had to put on while he raped me. All of those memories flooded me, but Cindy got me through it, she was so gentle and never seemed to judge me at any point. After the interview, I felt such relief. I told Cindy and Steve about the evidence I had given many years before and they said they'd find the files. They'd disappeared. I didn't even have my copy that the counsellor from the support group had given me as I'd burned them. I was looking at them all the time and wondering how in the world the CPS could have chosen not to prosecute when it all seemed so clear, how they could have taken Dad at his word when I was talking of what a child had endured.

I decided at that point that I only needed to do one thing. Tell the truth. If I did that, I'd never be tripped up. He would, but I wouldn't. The truth is the truth. The files would have helped as they would have corroborated that truth over the years, but they were gone – I have no idea how – and I had Cindy and Steve on my side now. They checked in on me and kept me up to date all the time, even telling me when they were going to arrest Dad. They were going to his home at night and he would be taken in for questioning. I didn't hear anything until a few weeks later when Steve called me with news that my house was on red alert. One of my family members had been going to counselling and they had said that they were going to kill me for saying such things about Dad, as it would affect their reputation too. The counsellor was horrified, and believed it to be a credible threat, so he had called the police. With the real possibility that my house was going to be set on fire, I had a decision to make about the safety of my youngest child. I asked Max's dad if he would look after him while all this went on as he was only 5. We agreed it was temporary so that I could focus on the court case which had overtaken my life, and not be left with the terror that my little boy would be burned to death in his bed one night. I wanted justice but not at the expense of my baby.

In May 2013, I received a letter which was headed 'Notice to attend Crown Court.' I looked at the sheet of paper which had the hard, indisputable charges against my father in black and white. This was it. It was real and it was happening. He had pled not guilty to 6 counts of indecent assault, 11 counts of rape, 2 counts of indecency with a child, and one account of buggery.

When the day of the court date came, I was given witness protection. Jackie and I would be giving evidence in a separate room. There would be a cleared court and a screen so I didn't have to see him. When Jackie came back from the room, she was visibly upset.

'That was like being thrown into a lion's den and stripped naked,' she told me. She'd been in for hours, and still had more to go. We were told to go for lunch before the session restarted and told where to find the café. I was still feeling positive. I got my tray, started walking to the food area and froze. Sitting in front of me at a table was Dad. I hadn't seen him for 20 years. I couldn't move, it was as if my feet were stuck to the floor. Someone, I can't even remember who, ushered me away but I was terrified. To see him, to see his face and those eyes which had bored right into me again – why was that allowed to happen? It was so wrong that there was only one café there and I couldn't have been the first this had happened to. I seemed to be compiling a list of all the things that were wrong with this process, all the things which undermined the experience of the innocent.

Later that night, once the terror and fear had gone, I realised that, in some ways, I could see it as empowering. He was old, he wasn't the same man of my nightmares. His hair was white rather than really dark, and, although he was fat and heavy, he looked weak. I was the strong one now. When I had been in that café, I'd realised that there's not just fight or flight in response to fear, there's freeze too and that's the state I had been in for years.

Jackie gave her evidence for a day and a half, then it was my turn. I could see the judge, twelve jurors and a barrister from behind my screen. I'd only met my barrister the day before, and my first impression was that I wasn't sure about him. He just asked me to say what happened, in my own words. I wasn't far in before we finished for the day. As we got out, there was an ambulance and when we asked security, they said that our grandfather was struggling to breathe. He was 82 at that point – we were later told we'd struggle to find a jury that would convict an 82-year-old. I believe he was advised to feign it, but that's just my own personal opinion. He'd had no health problems before, but all of a sudden, he was at death's door. That night I just thought of what I'd face the next day. It was terrifyingly intimidating and the only way I got through those dark hours was by doing jigsaws. I became quite the expert at those over the course of the trial.

When I went in the next day, I could hear from speakers that people were murmuring about someone struggling to breathe. It was Grandfather in an oxygen mask. Let's just say, he's not dead yet. I only cried once as I gave all my evidence, again when I was speaking about that day that broke me. Otherwise, I was telling twelve strangers everything that had been done to me with no emotion at all. I felt thrown to wolves by Dad's defence barrister.

'You're nothing more than a fantasist, aren't you? Why are you lying about everything? This is all in your head, isn't it?' I was devastated. Someone had killed herself after a trial the year before after having those same words thrown at her and it wasn't supposed to be an approach any longer. I knew he had a job to do, but he went too far; it's just not right, how they question sexual abuse victims.

When we were almost done for the day, I heard a kerfuffle in the courtroom. I'd no idea what was going on as the Court was cleared and I was taken into a back room. Grandfather had collapsed in front of the jury and was taken to hospital again. I had a bad feeling about that, about the effect it could have on the jury, but we'd done our bit, it was now up to the police to do theirs. I was advised to stay away from court as the other witnesses took the stand. I have no idea what any of them, including Mum, said, but I do think that being told to go home and wait was a bad idea. It took ten days before the jury went out, but that hadn't been long enough for them to make a decision. When I got the call to go back to court, I genuinely thought we'd won – when we were told they couldn't reach a decision on either case, I could have collapsed. Our barrister had wanted a unanimous decision, but we couldn't even get a majority. I think they'd lost sight of us and they only had an ill, old grandfather in their minds. I also believe we should have been brought back again at the end to emphasise what had happened to us as children.

We were both completely devastated. Jackie had a panic attack so severe that the paramedics thought she was having a heart attack. My heart was so heavy and it felt broken again.

That night, I went to see my GP and told him that I didn't think I could go on. I cried until there were no tears left and I stopped naturally.

'I can't do this any more,' I told him. 'I can't do a retrial, I can't have people telling me I'm a liar again.'

'You've come this far,' he said, kindly. 'Why give up now?'

That man gave me the strength to believe that, yes, I could fight again. I called Cindy and Steve and said, 'Get it booked in as soon as you can; I'm going for another round.' They did and a month later, the case went back to court. During that time, my details had gone to a neighbour listing all the charges I had brought in detail. Another thing that should never have happened, another thing to add to my list. Who was talking about me in the street? I was so paranoid that everyone knew all these things about me behind my back, but I had to be strong and move on. Apart from there being twelve new jurors, the only difference with the retrial was that Grandfather wasn't going to be there. His alleged crimes would stay on file, but he was 82 and 'dying' so there was a decision made not to push it. It was the lesser of two evils for me – better than him being found innocent.

It was the same routine to begin with – Jackie first, then me. I found it easier as I knew what to expect. Jigsaws were still getting me through the night, and I used to play Uno in the waiting room with Jackie, focusing on winning, focusing on beating everyone! I definitely stayed away from the café.

When it was time for me to be cross-examined, the same barrister threw the same accusations at me again. *You're lying. You're a fantasist. This is all made up.* He had a new angle now: 'You also accused your grandfather, didn't you, but he isn't standing here today.' I couldn't argue with that and I also couldn't say that I thought he was putting it all on.

Back in the witness protection room, it only seemed to be a matter of minutes before my barrister came in, sat down, took his wig off and said the jury had been discharged.

'Why?' I asked. 'What does that mean?'

'It's because of what you said,' he told me.

'What do you mean?'

'Because of the evidence you gave, and because you were clearly telling the truth, your father wouldn't get a fair trial.'

'Are you joking?' I shouted. 'You have to tell the truth in a court of law! How can I be punished for that?' To this day, I can't understand how telling the truth is used against you. I made them go over all the documents to show what had happened, but it made no sense. He said I could have another retrial, but that was something I couldn't face.

'Wait, just wait . . .' he said, and went to speak with the Judge. Apparently, he'd heard me shouting and said that, if I did want a new trial, I would still have him in charge, he wouldn't allow another judge to take over. My barrister said that wasn't acceptable as he couldn't risk me getting ripped apart again for nothing and he felt it would be prejudicial against me if the same person heard my story for the third time.

'Don't give up,' he told me, and kept trying. He was in and out about half a dozen times but finally told me he'd found a slot in three weeks. He'd come through for me after all. I could hold on. What was the worst that could happen? That would be my last shot though, I couldn't spend my life doing this, especially since Max had now been away from me for five months.

The retrial followed the same process as before.

'It was your fantasy, wasn't it?' he told me.

That was sick. 'If I'd had a fantasy as a child, it would have been playing with dolls and living in a fairy castle, it would have been going to my little cottage and listening to the waves crash.' Dad's barrister used the same lines over and over again, but this Judge told him to move on.

Jackie and I decided not to step away this time and went back every day. The jurors saw us stand there every morning when we went in and every afternoon when they came out. When all of the evidence had been given again, when all of the cross-examination had been done again, the jury went out. The following afternoon, the Judge asked if they had reached a decision.

It's hard to explain how I felt at that point. I knew I couldn't do it again. I felt like I was at a crossroads. I would either move on with my life or never be able to progress, all depending on what twelve strangers said in the next few minutes. My heart was pounding, I was almost crying with the stress of it all, but then I heard the most wonderful thing.

Count 1, we find the defendant guilty.

Count 2, we find the defendant guilty.

By count 3, I was crying so much that I couldn't hear and I left the room, but it kept going. He was guilty. He was guilty. I'd always known it, but now the world did too. Jackie told me I should have stayed for the bit when the Judge said, 'take him down,' but I was delirious anyway. Not all of the counts had been addressed at that point, but when the jury came back in later that afternoon, the most wonderful thing happened – they'd found Dad guilty on 32 counts and he was sentenced to 15 years imprisonment. The charges and individual sentencing made such a shocking list that it was hard to believe they related to me.

Rape 28 November 1979 to 29 November 1980, 15 years imprisonment

Rape 28 November 1980 to 29 November 1983, 15 years imprisonment concurrent

Rape 28 November 1980 to 28 November 1983, 15 years imprisonment concurrent

Rape 17 November 1979 to 18 November 1980, 15 years imprisonment concurrent

Rape 17 November 1980 to 18 November 1980, 15 years imprisonment concurrent

Rape 17 November 1981 to 18 November 1982, 15 years imprisonment concurrent

Rape 17 November 1982 to 18 November 1983, 15 years imprisonment concurrent

Rape 17 November 1982 to 18 November 1983, 15 years imprisonment concurrent

Rape 17 November 1983 to 18 November 1984, 15 years imprisonment concurrent

Rape 17 November 1985 to 18 November 1986, 15 years imprisonment concurrent

Buggery 17 November 1983 to 18 November 1984, 15 years imprisonment concurrent

Committing gross indecency with a child 17 November 1978 to 18 November 1979, 3 years imprisonment concurrent

Committing gross indecency with a child 28 November 1979 to 18 November 1983, 3 years imprisonment concurrent

Indecent assault on a female 17 November 1979 to 18 November 1980, 3 years imprisonment concurrent

Indecent assault on a female 28 November 1979 to 29 November 1980, 3 years imprisonment concurrent

Indecent assault on a female 28 November 1979 to 29 November 1981, 3 years imprisonment concurrent

Indecent assault on a female 17 November 1983 to 18 November 1984, 18 months imprisonment concurrent

Indecent assault on a female 17 November 1983 to 29 November 1984, 18 months imprisonment concurrent

Indecent assault on a female 17 November 1982 to 18 November 1983, 18 months imprisonment concurrent

Defendant disqualified from working with children

To sign the Sex Offenders' Register for life

The total amount of imprisonment is 15 years.

It had actually been the same judge after all and I think that worked in my favour. He'd heard my unchanged story three times, and he'd heard Dad alter his on every occasion. It wasn't about the punishment − although it was right that he should have to pay − it was the acknowledgement. The Judge read out our impact statements and said, 'There are family loyalties but there are also things you cannot stand by and accept.' I wonder if my mum heard those words and realised that they applied to her?

I went outside to have a cigarette and try to calm my pounding heart. My barrister appeared at my side and said, 'Give me a fag, will you Scarlett?'

'I didn't know you smoked!' I told him.

He smiled. 'I didn't until today. This case, this case . . .' he just shook his head. When Dad's barrister came out, he had the temerity to try and shake my hand. I turned my back on him – how could he even sleep at night?

I went home and all I could think of was getting Max back. He had started school where Jimmy lived, but after he spent the summer holidays with me, that would change as it had always been a temporary arrangement.

'You're joking, aren't you?' Jimmy told me. 'No, he's my son and he's coming back here.' Over the summer, I just thought he'd been silly and would be backing down, but three days before school began, I received a letter to say a family court emergency meeting had been arranged for that Monday. Jimmy had put in allegations that Max was in danger of harm from me and his one bit of evidence was that, on one day of the week when he had stayed at home, I hadn't managed to take Max to playgroup. That was it, that was all he had. He wasn't even on the birth certificate but he was trying to steal my son. I sent a letter asking for them to delay any meeting – it was the weekend and my son was due to start school on the Monday.

To whom it may concern

I, Scarlet Jones, have received court papers that are stating I need to be in Plymouth Court on Monday. I am requesting an adjournment to be made to seek legal advice on this matter as I don't feel confident enough to face the court system alone. As I have only had today to respond to this, I have been unsuccessful in finding a solicitor that can see me. I request a new hearing be set to give me adequate time to speak with someone who understands the court procedure and can advise me on what I need to do. I have sole parental responsibility at present and the applicant has chosen not to put his name on the birth certificate. Max is not in any way at harm, nor would he ever be in my care. I have Max's best interests at heart and always have. Being here with me, his two sisters, his brother, nieces, nephews, and extended family offers Max the best place to be. He has always asked to come back and live with us here and it was Max's own decision to do that – this is what he wants and needs. He has had 7, almost 8, weeks of knowing he is staying here and has settled back in perfectly. I believe that to try and make him return would be totally detrimental to him and the happiness and stability that he now has. His father has moved with him four times in the last two years – I can promise I would never do that.

I could only hope it would have some effect. I waited that whole weekend, biting my nails and wondering if they would get back to me. I would do anything to keep my little boy. They could put any conditions on that they wanted. I heard nothing.

On Tuesday I got a call to say that Jimmy had been awarded full parental custody. I had 48 hours to send him back or I'd be arrested. My letter was never put in front of that family court judge. Max was screaming the next day at the thought of going back to Jimmy, who didn't even have the decency to come and get him, sending his brother in his place to prise my son's hands from the door. I'd only sent him away as protection from the death threats and now I'd lost him – had I traded my son for the guilty verdict against my dad?

I found a solicitor who was willing to take my case on, but I then had to deal with CAFCASS – has anyone ever had a good story to tell about them? They ignored so much in their so-called report. Max was allowed out on his own to wander the streets when he got back. He was given a social media account when he was 6. They lost him at the playground. I found out that Jimmy had a record. None of it mattered. They halved my contact. What CAFCASS and that court did to me was worse than any of the abuse and rapes. It was like being abused all over again.

They've taken your baby, Scarlett, but you know how hard you can fight. You also know that children grow up – they grow and they learn, they see who loves them and who harms them. Max has something you never had; he has a mother who loves him and who will fight like a tiger. Keep loving him and he will come back to you, always

be truthful with him and he will see who you are.
Hold onto that, hold onto the fact that telling the
truth has finally worked in one part of your life.
You spoke out and you were believed; now you
just have to wait.

Chapter Fourteen

Fight to win

I spent the next few years fighting. I fought for Max, and I fought CAFCASS and the system. First of all, I focused on the problems I had seen during the trial. The fact that I'd had to face my father in the café when I was due to give evidence against him was something I never wanted anyone to have to experience again. I contacted my MP who wrote to the Minister of State for Policing, Crime, Criminal Justice and Victims. It was a long title for a body whose response suggested they were completely toothless. They replied with vague words about appreciating that meeting my father in the café must have been 'upsetting.' The solution? Email the Crown Court, check a website about complaints, rest assured that the government is 'committed to putting victims and witnesses first.' Really? To face your abuser like that is completely unacceptable and repeating impersonal manifesto pledges didn't cut it in the slightest. My MP said in an additional letter to me, 'I appreciate that more effort should have been made to make you aware of procedure.' I felt that I was being told to move on, just as I had been so many times before.

At every step of the way, I had faced people who were in denial or who thought I didn't matter, and they were the ones who colluded in my abuse. When I was a child, when I was a teenager, then a young woman, then someone going through depression, then someone who had her son taken from her after a court system had tried to break her again, I have had so little help.

It's hard to get on with your life when everything you could have been is taken from you. I begged for help for so long, but there's nothing. After Dad was convicted, I had to make a choice – should I also try to make Ed pay for what he had done? I decided against it, because, for me, it was Dad who had groomed me in the first place. If he hadn't done those awful things, I wouldn't have been primed for what happened next. He made it possible. I thought I had been put on Earth for this. I'd been raped since I was eight years old and it was my normal. What he had done to me ran deep – he had actually prepared me for others, the foundations were in place. He had made me think that was all I was good for. I did want Ed to face justice, but I also knew that there were things going on in Telford that I could never battle. There were more and more rumours that young girls were being targeted in their hundreds, if not thousands. It was different to what had happened to me – I thought – but the fact that the police still seemed so disinterested made me feel that my fight against Dad had been the vital one.

Of course I reflect, of course I do. Not everyone got out. Some of the girls from my generation are still in it, one way or another – often with daughters who have seen no different, who think all of that is normal. I know that Kirstin – one of the friends who was hung over a bridge to threaten her after she was with me when I broke curfew – got an Asian boyfriend after that. He battered seven shades of shit out of her as well. It was a really common situation to have a Pakistani boyfriend back then, and it's something that is still the way. When I started working with Holly and began to hear the life stories of young women, there had been few changes in the strategies the perpetrators used. They are still so flattering to teenagers with spots and raging hormones. They are told they are beautiful for the first time. While the white boys tell them how ugly they are, the Asian lads have cars and a perfected technique of flattery; they always look smart and they become a status boyfriend. They made you think you were in a relationship, but it was a dictatorship. There was always an age gap too. All of this became very common very quickly until it was out of control in Telford. Girls still haven't been taught different, or boys – now, white boys have adopted the same techniques as they saw them working.

I do have flashbacks. Of the houses that all looked the same, the houses that weren't homes, that were just rape rooms. Every time I pass the mosque in Wellington, I remember that was the one they all went to and that Wellington was one of the places I was taken most often by Ed and his friends. I never saw other girls when they took me to those places – they used the segregation to their advantage – but I knew that I wasn't the only one living that sort of life.

I've passed a house where I was once taken by Ed just after I had Danny. There were two men in the kitchen and they all started chatting in Urdu and laughing when we walked in. I was behind him, so nervous and fully aware of what was coming. I lived in constant fear. One of them indicated for me to follow him. They were in their late 30s at least, and smelled so bad, the whole house did; they sweated that stench out of their pores. I was taken into one of the two front rooms which had a couple of filthy mattresses on the floor as usual. He never spoke English, just gestured for me to get onto the mattress and to take off my clothes. I lay down, wanting it over and done with. Quicker I let him, quicker I'd get out. I could still hear laughing and chatting between Ed and the other man in the kitchen. It was all so normalised. I disappeared in my mind, he finished, but as I tried to get dressed the other one came in and I had to start again. I had no feelings by that stage in my life. I just always knew I had to do it. I never know how I will react going past one of those houses, but I do always wonder if there is another girl on a mattress in there.

As an adult, getting feelings back has been so hard. The more people tell you you're a dirty slag, the more you believe it. I would ask myself, how dare I think I'm ever any more than that? I still can't take a compliment or accept any nice words ever. I'd leave them, their semen dripping from me and think, *I am what they say I am*.

I remember being raped in a graveyard once, literally on a gravestone. After he left, I sat crying, thinking why wouldn't men leave me alone? I had no escape, everyone knew who and what I was. I was easy, I was dirty. I had been physically, mentally and emotionally groomed for years. I was fair game. The nice moments I held onto with Ed were very few – he knew what he was doing, he'd throw me scraps. It's learned behaviour through generations. Somebody in their lives – everyone – tells them white girls are worthless and that allows them to completely dehumanise us. I'd had to be a good girl for Dad, I still just wanted to please, so I was a good girl for Ed too, even though he didn't even see me as a person.

When I went through the process of coming to terms with my past, it dawned on me that the paternal side of my family was riddled with abuse. When Jackie told of the horrors she had been put through by our grandfather, I had thought that was her story. The truth was, although he hadn't raped me, he had abused me too. When we had to go visit our grandparents, there were often the little things that happened. We went for Christmases, Easters, things like that, to their great big house. They had a massive shed outside, it was the size of a smaller house really, and it had big chest freezers. Gran would tell me to go out and get myself an ice-cream but Grandfather was always stood where I had to walk down the side of the freezer. I couldn't get past him, and he didn't move, so he would always touch me when I tried to squeeze past. This became a regular thing. He'd put his hand down my trousers or up my dress, whatever I had on, and he'd always be sneaky when he went past me. In the kitchen, he'd grab me or touch me, that type of thing, from as far back as I can remember. He would have been in his 50s at that point, a scruffy man with dirty hands who was frequently doing odd jobs that involved digging or laying concrete. I remember that because his hands were so rough when he touched me, the callouses rubbing on my skin.

Once, when I was about 12, I was sent there to stay the night and, the next morning, he drove me back home. He had this horrible old Morris Minor with a wooden frame, which I hated but I don't know if I always did or whether it was because of the association after that drive. He pulled into a layby on a country lane and said, 'You know what you have to do,' he said, winking – it's only now that I realise he and Dad must have been talking about it. There were quite a few brothers in that family and I reckon only one of them wasn't a pervert; in fact, as soon as he had his own kid he moved away, so I reckon he knew what the others were like. At the trial, I could empathise with Jackie, but I knew my experiences with our grandfather were nothing compared to hers – how awful is that?

Jackie and I have been through court and everyone assumes we know each other's horrors, but I don't know what happened to her and she doesn't know what happened to me. It's quite hard when you've got your own shit you have to deal with. He was definitely abusing her more, because she had to stay there more than I did, but we haven't really spoken about the whole scale of it. I know she has this sense of guilt that I tell her she doesn't need to own, because it's not her guilt to carry that she didn't do anything else. I wish I could take my own advice on things.

Another thing I realise when I look back is that – it sounds stupid – but so much of the abuse, with Dad and Ed, was incredibly repetitive and mundane, because it happened so many times. You even get used to your lip being split or being unable to go to the toilet because you have yet another infection, when it happens all the time. It was the same thing over and over again, which is quite sad in itself. It simply became my life; the same life with Dad, then the same again with Ed.

My children always knew what had happened to me, not all of the details, but they knew I was abused as a child – they were given that information in an age-appropriate way because obviously I've had bad days, and they needed to know why. My kids supported me all through the court case, so it's something I've never hid from them, but Lola has always been particularly informative about it.

One day, she brought me a book she'd been reading.

'Mum,' she said. 'You need to have a look at this. The woman who wrote it, Holly, went through the same things as you – you should get in touch with her.'

I took it from her and started it straight away. After a few pages, I had to stop as it was so familiar. Everything I had been through with Ed and his friends had happened to Holly – but twenty years later. It was like reliving that part of my life. How could it have been going on so long, why had no one stopped it at any point?

I sent an email to Holly saying, *my daughter's read your book and said I need to contact you because this happened to me too.* I didn't expect much but a response came in almost immediately asking if I wanted to meet up. We decided to meet at a local conference for child sexual abuse, and I'm not sure it went that well to be honest! We chatted about our lives but I've got a resting bitch face at the best of times, so I would definitely be looking at her as if to say, *I don't really like you.* My face doesn't always match what I'm feeling as I did actually really like her! I'm not horrible, it's just how I protect myself, until I get to know somebody then they can know there's a gooey little person inside. I did like her, she just didn't know this.

Once she saw behind that growl, we realised that we'd been put through the same methods, the same abuse, the same relationships. We also worked out that they were all related to each other; Telford is quite a small town so we knew who the families were, recognised the surnames and linked it all up pretty quickly.

Holly was already halfway through her campaign to get an enquiry into CSE in Telford and I knew I wanted to support her every step of the way. I'd never take Ed to court but this could be a route into making sure that my story was heard, alongside the stories of the thousands of other girls who had been groomed and trafficked over the years. I went to Holly's house for coffee one day and saw this big plan on her wall, laying out what she wanted to do for survivors.

'I know what I needed,' I told her, 'and none of it was in place.' I started adding to it, and that's how the Holly Project was born. She already had the outline, and between us, we decided what was needed, the stuff we lacked and the support we lacked. It was all about understanding it from the inside and having someone to say, 'I know how you feel, I've been there too.' I was behind Holly 100% but it was definitely her achievement, she's an amazing woman. The fight for the enquiry was finally successful and began in March 2020.

I gave my evidence in an anonymous room that they'd hired in Telford – the locations have to keep changing because obviously a perpetrator could be sat outside.

There were just two people there, the person asking the questions and the person writing everything down. I was prepared, I knew what was coming. It took four and a half hours and they really did try to make the point that everyone's evidence matters, it doesn't matter if it was Joe Bloggs on the street or if it was your Nan in the window that saw something, everybody needs to give this evidence.

It's beyond belief that it is still happening now as it happened to me all those years ago. As much as the violence was bad for me, it's nothing compared to the violence now. As far as the pimping side goes, I don't know how much further it can go, it's so awful – there have been 5 deaths we know of in Telford alone and there was the awful case of a girl called Lucy Lowe who had her home torched by her abuser. There are drug overdoses and there are disappearances; I know that I would have done anything to get out of my own life at times, and that stands for so many. It's an epidemic and I don't care what anyone says, there are known tactics and it's being ignored.

Women are coming through our doors and I'm hearing of broken bones, forced abortions, and threats to rape little sisters and mums. I know of stories where CCTV is given to the police of it happening and no further action has been taken – how on earth can that be justified?

We need to combine going back to the basics, doing something about these houses with nothing but mattresses that are still there, but also recognising it's all about the money and technology is playing a big part nowadays. Grooming and trafficking girls is a huge business; you can see them in their big cars and their big houses. The bigger these are, the more respect and status they have in their own community even though, as always it's on the backs and knees of girls like me.

They've also moved on to college girls in the last few years as awareness has grown of the under-age trade. If they are over-16, the abusers can't be done for a criminal offence – so they get them as soon as possible at that age, particularly the ones who look even younger. They only need to make the first contact, then it can all be done through their phones, in chatrooms and in online groups. They know that we're watching for them, so once the first little bit of grooming is over with and they have the girl's number, it's as simple as 'get your arse down here now,' when they want them to be somewhere. The waiting outside schools is a bit of a myth nowadays because they're not stupid, they know that's what people are looking for, they know that the cameras are there.

Holly and I have so many more ideas, so many campaigns we want to get out there. This is my life's work. Speaking to the enquiry did draw a line under some of it for me as did the trial – both parts of my abuse had been listened to. This though, this book, is another level. I'm in charge of every single word and I can't tell you the power which comes from that.

I'm doing so well now and I've made a life I can be proud of, but it doesn't happen overnight. Since I got justice, I've changed my life; since I met Holly, I've found what I want to achieve through helping others. I know what my aspirations and dreams are now, and I know that I am strong enough to do anything I put my mind to. I could never understand, 'why me?' I could never understand how all of this could happen to one person. Now I know that what is done to you, what others choose to do to you, doesn't define you – it can build you, but it is only one part of who you are. I'm the woman I am because of it. I'm a fighter and I got through it all. I'm stronger than

I thought I could ever be – and I won't stop shouting to have my voice heard about the epidemic of abuse that is a cancer in our society.

I have read some of the stories of other survivors who were used for sex but who got presents or money; all I got was pure violence. I don't mean that presents or money would have made any difference, but Ed had managed to control me totally just through beating. When he hit me, he looked pure evil, teeth gritted, veins popping out of his forehead. I thought he'd kill me and, as no one cared about me anyway, it would be no loss. He had 'girlfriends' everywhere but would always say I was his, just to give me that tiny bit of hope. He had connections everywhere. After he broke the injunction, I called the police, and watched him stand outside chatting to them, laughing as they shook his hand. How do you fight that? He's been in prison now for money laundering, which shows just how much he had.

I want people who, like myself, have lost many years, to know the power of their story. There is life after this shit. There is life. It can be happy, it can be okay. And if it can bring closure to one person to understand that what happened actually wasn't her fault then that's good enough for me. I have my children and that's all that matters really. Max came back to me after all, just as I'd always hoped – he saw the lies and manipulation that were being used against him, and he saw my love. I think that's the message of all of this really. You can go through Hell, you can go through things that no one should ever experience, but if you can have moments of pure love, hold onto them.

I don't really 'do' feelings very well, but I am blessed with some of the people I have in my life now and they will give me the courage to keep battling for others, for all the little Scarletts out there. I'll keep fighting, and now that I have a taste for it, I'll fight to win, because after all, girls can change the world.

Little Scarlett – I am sorry for ignoring you for so long. You wanted and needed acknowledgment for all the pain you had been put through, and I thought I could drink it away, I thought I could fix it by having no feelings. What they did to you was incomprehensible and I know now why you struggled so long to accept that they were fully to blame. As a child you believed what you were told, as all children do. But you are safe now, no one will ever harm you again. I learnt so much from you about how to protect myself, how to not let myself be hurt again, how to show no emotion because no one is to know that I am dying inside. I still don't really know how to let the barriers down now to give someone a chance, but I'm trying and I do think I will find love one day. You protected me, you got me through, you helped me survive. Now it's time for me to show you that we are safe, we don't need those barriers. You can be exactly who you wanted to be, you can have fun and enjoy life. I want that little girl part of me back again. I want to laugh genuinely, I want to be able to believe that I deserve love and I deserve happiness. I need to say goodbye to you now, little Scarlett, because we've reached the end of this part of our journey. We're not separate, I'm not looking at you and seeing a different part of me – we're both that girl, this woman. We didn't choose this path, but we walked it – now, let's make the rest of the journey together. Let's walk towards the light and get the life we have wanted for so long. We deserve it. x

Epilogue

I have never really known whether anyone would want to read my story – I still don't! – but I've known for a long time that I wanted to tell it. As I write this, I'm wondering who you are. You know so much about me, things I thought I would never tell another living soul, but *who* have I told them to?

If you are someone who has never been touched by these issues, someone who has picked up the book because it caught their eye, the first thing I want to say to you is that I'm glad. I'm glad you had a childhood that was allowed to be a childhood, that you had teenage years which were fun, that you had relationships which made you feel good. I don't mean that in any sarcastic way at all. I'm genuinely happy for you. Every girl, every woman should have that but it's rare. There is an epidemic of violence towards women and girls out there, and it needs to be addressed. By reading my story, I hope that you open your eyes to it. Look out for the child who was me, look out for the girl who was me – and if you meet women like me, listen to what they have to say and do all you can to help. If you work with children, never lose your focus, never lose your grip on safeguarding. Teachers, medical professionals, everyone needs to watch for the quiet child and the disruptive child as you never know how it will present. Don't assume the child will tell you and don't assume that they don't love their abuser. Never be afraid to report any suspicions, and never feel that you are a busybody. Children rely on the eyes of the adults around them – make sure you're looking.

If you are reading this book because it has some resonance with your own experiences, then I hope you can see that it was never your fault. You don't have to spend the rest of your life paying the price for the things your abuser did to you.

Just remember this – *it was never you.*

It was never your fault.

It wasn't what you wore.

It wasn't what you said.

It wasn't how you looked.

You weren't old for your age or knowing for your age.

You didn't ask for it, you didn't beg for it.

You didn't manipulate or flirt.

There wasn't a wrong street to walk down.

There wasn't a wrong gang to hang around with.

There wasn't a way you looked at him that sent a message which said it was fine for him to do what he did.

It was never you.

Abusers choose to abuse. Rapists choose to rape. They aren't driven by lust or desire, they make their own choices. They also lie because they can. They lie because, all too often, society doesn't want to look at the truth. It's much easier to say she was wearing a short skirt – ignoring the girls in jeans, the women in hijab, the babies in nappies. If society looked at why men do this, they would have to look at why they are *allowed* to do it. Why the authorities, the police, the courts would rather rip a victim apart than ask why there is an epidemic of abuse in the world.

While writing my story, I felt that it was so important to reflect at the end of each chapter on what had happened and what I wish I had known. Age brings wisdom but I still wish there was a way to tell my younger self, *tell someone what has happened. People will still ignore you and pretend it's all you and your fault, but that says more about them than you. Someone will hear you eventually, and you need to hold on to that.*

I felt like the whole world was against me for so long, for far too long. Why did it keep happening? Why me again? What had I done to deserve these things? I think that is common for all victims, for all survivors, but remember: the one thing you always seemed to minimise was that it wasn't your fault, it was theirs. How were you ever going to know what a real healthy relationship looked like when you had never experienced one?

Looking back, I wish you could have screamed, shouted, fought to get the anger out of you before letting it consume you and everything you did, but you can't change the past, you can only stop it ruining your future. I was innocent when all of this started, and what my father did made sure I would never feel any freedom until now really. I am proud of me, of who I have become, and of the fact that I did it despite them. I know that I still need to work on not being too hard on myself and not being mad at me for how I have often reacted. I must hold on to what I have achieved, to the conviction, my children, and the work I do.

If you are reading this because you are still in it, please get help when you are ready to. Tell someone you trust, get to a refuge, find a place of safety – but do it on your terms. No one has the right to tell you to go to the police or to say that if you don't, you are betraying others who might be abused too. I'll repeat again – the abuser chooses to abuse. You will find your time and you will find your power. There are groups out there – like The Holly Project – who will listen and who will take the steps with you that make you comfortable. We are there, just as others are there, and if my book has achieved one thing, I hope it is to make you realise that you can be the woman you want to be. It might take a long time, just as it did for me, but you can get there.

You have survived this so far.

Keep surviving and find out what your story is.

Newport Community
Learning & Libraries

Acknowledgements

There are so many people to thank – I really hope that I haven't forgotten anyone, and that readers understand there are many who I can't name.

For my children – you mean the world to me. That is such a basic thing to say, and it's something that most people reading this will see as completely normal, but it isn't normal for the abused. Their normal, as I hope I've helped you understand, is something completely different. So, to all of you, what I want more than anything for you is to have my love in a way that is a million miles from what I experienced. I love you with all my heart and you make my life worth living.

I want to thank my ghostwriter, Linda Watson-Brown, for talking to me for hours on end, for listening, and making me feel that my story was worth it. For finding our wonderful editor Ajda Vucicevic at Mirror Books, and for never doubting that my voice needed to be heard.

I want to thank not just the lovely Ajda, but the whole team at Mirror Books. There are so many people behind this that I have never met, but I want them all to know how much I appreciate their hard work.

To 'H' for believing in me and showing me that I wasn't alone. You give me such strength and I'll never take it for granted.

To my best friends, Debbie and Becky – you have both given me shoulders to cry on and to lean on, you've picked me up when I've been at my lowest, and I couldn't wish for better, stronger women in my life.

For the YMCA, who gave us a chance when they knew it was a risk.

Acknowledgements

I'd like to give particular thanks to Steve Parton and Cindi Hendry, the police officers who became almost family to me.

I want to end by thanking someone who is no longer with us – my Auntie Cindy. She passed two years ago, but, as an adult, always offered me a safe place. She is missed more than I can say, but I know that she would be proud of me for finally finding my voice.

The Holly Project

The Holly Project is a free support service for survivors of Child Sexual Exploitation (CSE). It is an independent drop-in service that is run by survivors of CSE. It offers a safe place for individuals – and their families – to get support and advice from people who really understand the trauma and lasting impact of CSE. The Holly Project runs groups for survivors and victims as well as for families and parents.

You can email direct at:
hollyproject@ymcawellington.co.uk
or call on 01952 947831.

If you do get in touch, please don't try to guess who I am. I have stayed anonymous for a reason. And anyway – does it matter? I am your friend, your sister, your mother, your daughter, your co-worker, your teacher, your doctor, your neighbour.

I am you.